The Balanced Scorecard

Applications in Internal Auditing and Risk Management

Mark L. Frigo, PhD, CPA, CMA

Sponsored by

The Institute of
Internal Auditors
Chicago Chapter

Copyright © 2014 by The Institute of Internal Auditors Research Foundation (IIARF).

All rights reserved.

Published by The Institute of Internal Auditors Research Foundation
247 Maitland Avenue
Altamonte Springs, Florida 32701-4201

No part of this publication may be reproduced, stored in a retrieval system, or transmitted in any form by any means—electronic, mechanical, photocopying, recording, or otherwise—without prior written permission of the publisher. Requests to the publisher for permission should be sent electronically to: bookstore@theiia.org with the subject line "reprint permission request."

Limit of Liability: The IIARF publishes this document for informational and educational purposes and is not a substitute for legal or accounting advice. The IIARF does not provide such advice and makes no warranty as to any legal or accounting results through its publication of this document. When legal or accounting issues arise, professional assistance should be sought and retained.

The Institute of Internal Auditors' (IIA's) International Professional Practices Framework (IPPF) comprises the full range of existing and developing practice guidance for the profession. The IPPF provides guidance to internal auditors globally and paves the way to world-class internal auditing.

The IIA and The IIARF work in partnership with researchers from around the globe who conduct valuable studies on critical issues affecting today's business world. Much of the content presented in their final reports is a result of IIARF-funded research and prepared as a service to The IIARF and the internal audit profession. Expressed opinions, interpretations, or points of view represent a consensus of the researchers and do not necessarily reflect or represent the official position or policies of The IIA or The IIARF.

ISBN-13: 978-0-89413-876-8

18 17 16 15 14   2 3 4 5 6 7 8 9

Contents

Executive Summary vii
Acknowledgments ix
About the Author xi

Chapter 1:	Introduction	1
Chapter 2:	The Balanced Scorecard Framework	5
Chapter 3:	Strategy Maps	11
Chapter 4:	Guidelines for Using Balanced Scorecards to Manage and Measure Performance	15
Chapter 5:	Return Driven Strategy Framework	19
Chapter 6:	Mission Driven Strategy Framework	33
Chapter 7:	A Strategic GRC Framework	41
Chapter 8:	Developing a Balanced Scorecard for the Internal Audit Function	45
Chapter 9:	Using Strategy Maps for Risk Assessment and ERM	63
Chapter 10:	How to Conduct a Strategic Risk Assessment	71
Chapter 11:	Summary and Conclusions	83
Appendix A:	The IIA's Imperatives for Change	91
Appendix B:	History of the Balanced Scorecard	93

Notes 97

Glossary 103
Bibliography 105

The IIA Research Foundation Sponsor Recognition 113
The IIA Research Foundation Board of Trustees 117
**The IIA Research Foundation Committee of Research and
Education Advisors** 119

List of Figures

Figure 3.1:	Strategy Map: Cause-and-Effect Relationships Among Strategic Objectives	12
Figure 5.1:	Return Driven Strategy Framework	21
Exhibit 6.1:	Mission Driven Strategy for Internal Audit	34
Exhibit 7.1:	Strategic GRC Framework	42
Figure 8.1:	A Balanced Scorecard for Internal Audit	48
Figure 9.1:	Strategic Risk Management Framework	65
Figure 9.2:	Strategy Map with Embedded Risk Management Objectives	67
Figure 10.1:	Strategic Risk Assessment Process	72

Executive Summary

The Balanced Scorecard performance management system is widely used by organizations and has become a leading management framework for strategy execution throughout the world. A 2002 report from The Institute of Internal Auditors Research Foundation (IIARF) described early usage of Balanced Scorecards and Strategy Maps in internal auditing as a way to translate strategy into action and to manage and measure internal audit performance.

These Balanced Scorecard applications have continued as internal audit professionals have sought to develop their functions strategically. The internal audit strategy to focus on enterprise risk management (ERM) and risk assessment provides an opportunity to use Strategy Maps in risk assessment and risk management.

This book provides the necessary background information and terminology on the Balanced Scorecard and Strategy Maps to help ensure that internal auditors will gain an invaluable strategic skill set. It also describes management tools, strategy frameworks, and leading practices to assist internal auditors in applying the Balanced Scorecard framework and Strategy Maps.

Developing a Strategy for the Internal Audit Function

The first step in developing a Balanced Scorecard is designing a clear strategy that can then be translated into action. The book describes frameworks that can be used to develop and refine a strategy for an internal audit function. These frameworks also can be used to connect the internal audit function's strategy with that of the enterprise.

Developing a Balanced Scorecard for the Internal Audit Function

The Balanced Scorecard framework presented provides an overview of concepts and terminology. I also discuss approaches for developing a Balanced Scorecard for an internal audit function and incorporate some general examples.

Applications of the Balanced Scorecard and Strategy Maps in Risk Assessment and ERM

ERM is an excellent opportunity for internal auditors to apply Strategy Maps. The book describes the approaches for using the Balanced Scorecard and Strategy Maps in risk assessment and ERM.

Acknowledgments

I would first like to acknowledge The IIA's Chicago Chapter for generously sponsoring this research project and facilitating a roundtable discussion to gather insights from leading practitioners.

Many internal audit professionals and thought leaders contributed their ideas and insights to help develop this book, including:

    David Landsittel, former COSO Chairman
    Michael Pryal, *Federal Signal Corporation*
    Jeff Perkins, *TransUnion*
    Kathy Swain, *Allstate Insurance*
    Joe Steakley, *HCA Healthcare*
    Greg Kalin, *Morningstar*
    Paul Walker, *St. John's University*
    Larry Harrington, *Raytheon Company*
    Kathy Robinson, *ADP*
    James Alexander, *Unitus Community Credit Union*
    Edward Pitts, *Avago Technologies*
    John Covell, *General Growth Properties*
    Christy Rodriguez, *Caesars Entertainment*
    Brian Brown, *PricewaterhouseCoopers (PwC)*

I especially thank Dick Anderson, clinical professor at DePaul University, for his collaboration in developing many of the ideas in this book. I also give special thanks to Bob Kaplan from Harvard Business School for his thought leadership in developing the Balanced Scorecard framework (with David P. Norton).

The project could not have been done without the help of The IIA staff, especially Deborah Poulalion, and project team members from The IIA Research Foundation's Committee of Research and Education Advisors (CREA)—Debby Munoz, James Alexander, Michael Pryal (IIA Board of Trustees), Sabrina Hearn, and Warren Stippich.

The excellent editing by Deborah Poulalion and The IIA Research Foundation's team was especially valuable. Research Fellows from the Center for Strategy, Execution, and Valuation and Strategic Risk Management Lab at DePaul University were instrumental in conducting the chief audit executive workshop and developing the manuscript. They include Amy Frigo, Matthew Vladika, William Scherba, John Wesley, Wei Su, and Libo (Bob) Hou.

About the Author

Mark L. Frigo, PhD, CPA, CMA, is director of The Center for Strategy, Execution, and Valuation and the Strategic Risk Management Lab in the Kellstadt Graduate School of Business at DePaul University in Chicago and Ledger & Quill Alumni Foundation Distinguished Professor of Strategy and Leadership in the Driehaus College of Business at DePaul. Author of seven books and more than 100 articles, his work is published in leading business journals, including *Harvard Business Review*. Dr. Frigo is a member of the Duke Corporate Education network and lead instructor for the Center for Financial Leadership. He has developed and presented education courses in strategy, strategic risk management, and leadership strategy programs for universities, corporate universities, and professional organizations throughout North America, Asia-Pacific, and Europe.

Dr. Frigo received his bachelor of science degree in accountancy from the University of Illinois, an MBA degree from Northern Illinois University, and completed postgraduate studies in the Kellogg Graduate School of Management at Northwestern University. He received his PhD in econometrics. He is a certified public accountant (CPA) and a certified management accountant (CMA).

His professional career has included corporate strategic planning, mergers and acquisitions, and management consulting at KPMG. He is the three-time recipient of the Economos Distinguished Teaching Award in the Kellstadt Graduate School of Business, and has received numerous awards by professional organizations for his executive education programs. Please visit www.markfrigo.com for his latest research and publications.

Chapter 1

Introduction

The Balanced Scorecard was originally introduced in 1992 to improve corporate performance measurement by balancing lagging metrics of financial performance with nonfinancial metrics that drive future performance. Today, the Balanced Scorecard framework and Strategy Maps are extensively used by organizations worldwide and have become a leading management tool for strategy execution.

Many of internal auditing's best practices in performance measurement are consistent with the Balanced Scorecard approach. As a result, leading internal audit functions are using the Balanced Scorecard approach as a strategic performance management tool to add value to the organization. The Balanced Scorecard framework and Strategy Maps can help chief audit executives (CAEs) to:

- Describe and communicate the internal audit department's strategy

- Translate that strategy into strategic objectives and performance measures

- Develop performance measures for the internal audit function that are linked to organizational strategy

- Facilitate continuous improvement in the internal audit function

- Showcase the role and value of the internal audit function

- More effectively conduct strategic risk assessments

Recently, applying Strategy Maps as a platform for risk assessment is an approach that can be adapted by internal audit professionals in their risk assessment and risk management activities.[1]

This book explains the use of various frameworks, management tools, and other leading practices, including:

- The Balanced Scorecard framework
- Return Driven Strategy framework
- Mission Driven Strategy framework
- Strategic governance, risk, and compliance (GRC) framework
- Strategic risk management framework
- Strategic risk assessment process

Building on Previous Knowledge

My previous book, *A Balanced Scorecard Framework for Internal Auditing,* was published by The Institute of Internal Auditors Research Foundation (IIARF) in 2002. It was used by CAEs and internal auditors to develop Balanced Scorecards for internal audit functions. This book provides the latest developments in Balanced Scorecards and Strategy Maps. Extensive insights have been added based on a CAE roundtable hosted by The IIA's Chicago Chapter (December 2012) and feedback received from CAEs at leading organizations, including ADP, Allstate Insurance, Federal Signal Corporation, HCA Healthcare, Morningstar, Raytheon, St. John's University, TransUnion, Unitus Community Credit Union, and other organizations.

Benefits for Internal Audit Functions

This book will enable readers to confidently answer the following questions about strategy and performance measures for their internal audit functions:

Introduction

Strategy

- What is the strategy of your internal audit department?
- How well is the strategy understood within the internal audit department?
- How well is the strategy of the internal audit department understood by its constituents outside the department?
- How does internal audit create value for its constituents and stakeholders (board, audit committee, management, audit customers)?

Performance Measures

- How effectively do performance measures describe the strategy of your department?
- How closely are performance measures linked to your departmental strategy?
- How well are performance measures aligned with the organization's strategies and initiatives?
- Do performance measures include leading indicators, as well as lagging indicators?
- Are cause-and-effect linkages between performance measures clear?
- How effectively are performance measures used for continuous improvement?
- How effectively do performance measures provide a way to show the value of the department?
- How do performance measures for individuals and teams reflect the departmental strategy?
- How are departmental innovations and capabilities reflected in your existing performance measures?

Chapter 2

The Balanced Scorecard Framework

The Balanced Scorecard framework is a strategic performance measurement system for executing the strategy of an organization. It provides a pathway for translating an organization's mission and strategy into a set of actionable strategic objectives and performance measures.

Background

The Balanced Scorecard performance management system was introduced in 1992 by Robert S. Kaplan, Marvin Bower Professor of Leadership Development, Emeritus at Harvard Business School, and David P. Norton, founder of a number of consulting companies, including the Nolan-Norton Company, where the original Balanced Scorecard was developed.[1] They introduced the Balanced Scorecard in a January–February 1992 *Harvard Business Review* article, "The Balanced Scorecard: Measures that Drive Performance," and a 1996 book, *The Balanced Scorecard: Translating Strategy into Action*, that has been translated into 24 languages.[2] Their fifth and most recent book, *The Execution Premium: Linking Strategy to Operations for Competitive Advantage* (2008), captures the accumulated lessons from the previous 15 years and describes how the Balanced Scorecard has become the number one management system for strategy execution.[3] During the last 20 years, Kaplan and Norton have helped create a new body of knowledge, key terminology, and concepts for strategy execution that is now being used throughout the private, nonprofit, and public sectors.

The Balanced Scorecard framework comprises two powerful management tools: the Balanced Scorecard[4] and Strategy Maps.[5]

Focusing on Strategy

Since it was developed in the 1990s, the Balanced Scorecard framework has evolved from a performance measurement system to a strategy execution system.[6] By translating strategy into actionable terms and contributing to making strategy and its execution a continual process, the Balanced Scorecard has become the centerpiece of strategy execution in many organizations. It has been broadly adopted in a wide range of industries, as well as nonprofit and public sector organizations.

The Balanced Scorecard framework has been found to be useful and robust across various industries and across firms of different sizes.[7] Many organizations use this hierarchy or adapt it in some way. For nonprofit and public sector organizations, the architecture is modified to focus on the Mission Driven strategy, which is also described in this book.[8]

The Four Perspectives of the Balanced Scorecard

The strategic objectives and performance measures within the Balanced Scorecard framework are derived from the strategy of the organization. The Balanced Scorecard performance measures are generally organized in a hierarchy that considers four primary perspectives: financial, customer, internal business processes, and learning and innovation. Management can use the framework to connect the strategic business activities to the ultimate goal of creating financial value.

The four perspectives of the Balanced Scorecard framework provide the structure for addressing strategic objectives in cause-and-effect linkage with related performance measures. Linkages within the hierarchy can be powerful tools for strategy evaluation and refinement.[9] Generally, the cause-and-effect linkage among strategic objectives and performance measures starts with the learning and growth perspective, which drives internal process perspective performance, which, in turn, drives customer perspective performance, and ultimately drives performance in the financial perspective of the scorecard.

1. Financial Perspective

This perspective focuses on key financial performance of an organization. Strategic objectives and performance measures relating to return on investment, profitability, revenue growth, and other supporting financial performance are included here. Examples of performance measures in the financial perspective include operating income, return on invested capital, and annual revenue growth. The first tenet of business strategy is to ethically maximize financial value.[10]

The financial perspective should provide the organization with the right objectives and metrics to achieve its financial goals. This means having specific objectives and targets for key financial metrics.

2. Customer Perspective

Focusing on customer performance in areas that are most critical to the customer, this perspective includes broad objectives, such as improving customer satisfaction and customer retention, and other objectives related to specific customer needs and performance requirements. Customer performance will logically drive financial performance under the premise that the customer is the pathway to revenue growth.[11] Examples of performance measures include customer satisfaction and customer retention.

The customer perspective is based on the customer value proposition, which defines how the organization creates value for its customers and therefore how it creates financial value for its shareholders.[12] This means that customer performance measures must be aligned to the specific performance that customers demand, whether it is on-time delivery or a specific quality level of a product offering that the customer requires.

3. Internal Process Perspective

This perspective comprises internal business processes that drive customer performance, as well as ensure efficient and effective operations that directly support profitability and return on investment. At the heart of strategy execution, it includes performance measures on cost, quality, and time for processes that are critical to customers; in other words, the "cheaper/faster/better" mantra that refers to the cost, time, and quality performance within the internal processes. Examples of performance measures include cost per unit, number of defects, and cycle time.

The Balanced Scorecard framework's internal process perspective should consider the value chain of the organization as the sequence of business processes that add usefulness to the products or services of an organization, including innovation, operations, and post-sales processes.[13]

4. Learning and Innovation Perspective

Learning and innovation focus on performance objectives relating to employees, infrastructure, teaming, and capabilities necessary for internal processes. Examples of performance measures include employee satisfaction, hours of training per employee, and information technology expenditures per employee. This perspective focuses on translating intangible assets into tangible outcomes and encompasses human capital, information capital, and organization capital.[14]

Balanced Scorecard Terminology

The terminology for Balanced Scorecard includes strategic objectives, performance measures, baseline performance, target performance, and supporting strategic initiatives.

> **Strategic Themes.** Strategic themes generally involve growth and productivity. Both should be represented and described in the Balanced Scorecard. For example, a growth strategic theme could be to "grow revenue from international sales," and a productivity strategic theme might be to "improve asset utilization."
>
> **Strategic Objectives.** Strategic objectives describe the strategy of the organization and are included in the four perspectives of the Balanced Scorecard. They are statements of what the strategy must achieve and what is critical to success. An example of a growth strategic initiative's objective in the financial perspective would be to "increase revenue from new product offerings."
>
> **Performance Measures.** This Balanced Scorecard component describes how success in achieving the strategy will be measured and tracked for a particular strategic objective. An example of a performance measure is "percentage of total revenue from new product offerings."
>
> **Baseline Performance.** This represents the current level of performance. An example of a baseline performance for "percentage of total revenue from new product offerings" might be 15 percent.

Targets. The level of performance or rate of improvement needed is often represented by "stretch targets," which provide a goal that is challenging, yet attainable. An example of a target for "percentage of total revenue from new product offerings" would be 20 percent (as opposed to the 15 percent baseline).

Strategic Initiatives. Key action programs or action plans are required to achieve strategic objectives. These describe the details of the actions needed, timelines, responsibility assignments for each step, and resources necessary to achieve the initiatives. In short, strategic objectives focus on *what* is to be achieved, strategic initiatives focus on *how* it will be achieved, and performance measures, baseline performance, and targets relate to *measuring* the progress.

Characteristics of the Balanced Scorecard

- **Strategy focused.** Performance measures are driven by mission, vision, and strategy.

- **Balanced.** Performance measures are balanced in terms of financial and nonfinancial measures, leading and lagging measures, and internal (internal processes) and external (customer) measures.

- **Includes both financial and nonfinancial measures.** Performance measure include traditional financial measures, as well as nonfinancial measures.

- **Cause-and-effect linkages.** Performance measures are connected using cause-and-effect linkages, and include performance drivers (leading indicators) and outcome performance measures (lagging indicators).

- **Unique to the strategy.** Performance measures are unique and customized to an organization's strategy.

Chapter 3

Strategy Maps

Strategy Maps in the Balanced Scorecard framework are diagrams of the cause-and-effect relationships among strategic objectives.[1] For example, the Strategy Map in **figure 3.1** depicts linkage of strategic objectives across the four perspectives for a manufacturer. To "increase R&D and innovation investment" in the capabilities perspective drives the strategic objective to "develop new product offerings" in the internal process perspective, which in turn drives the efforts to "acquire new customers" and "increase profitability per customer" in the customer perspective, which ultimately drives "revenue growth" and "profitability" in the financial perspective. This can be referred to as the *vertical logic* of the Strategy Map.

The strategic objective to "develop new product offerings" refers to performance measures, such as "revenue from new products" and "margins from new products," which lead to target level of performance and initiatives or action plans, which support the achievement of the strategic objective. This can be referred to as the horizontal logic of the Strategy Map.

Following are examples of key strategic objectives and related performance measures, as viewed from each of the four perspectives:

Financial Perspective

Strategic Objective	Performance Measure
Increase return on investment	Return on investment
Revenue growth	Percent growth in revenue
Increase profitability	Net income as a percentage of sales

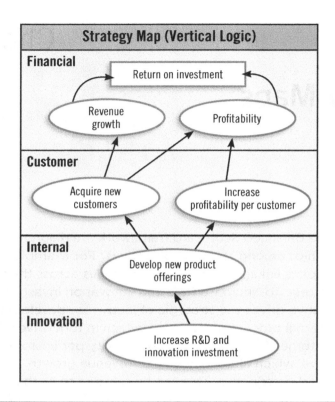

Figure 3.1. Strategy Map: Cause-and-Effect Relationships Among Strategic Objectives
Author's creation.

This financial perspective example relates to return on investment and the supporting measure of revenue growth and profitability.

Customer Perspective

Strategic Objective	Performance Measure
Increase customer satisfaction	Customer satisfaction ratings
Increase customer share	Revenue per customer
Attract new customers	Number of new customers Revenue from new customers

This customer perspective example includes some of the typical performance measures, including customer satisfaction and revenue per customer, as well as customer measures related to a growth strategy, such as number of new customers and resulting revenues.

Internal Business Processes Perspective

Strategic Objective	Performance Measure
Improve on-time delivery	Percentage of on-time deliveries
Improve quality performance	Number of rejects

This internal business processes example includes on-time delivery and quality, which are traditional measures for a manufacturing firm.

Learning and Growth Perspective

Strategic Objective	Performance Measure
Train employees on quality tools	Hours of training on quality tools

This learning and growth perspective example reveals some possible cause-and-effect relationships. Increasing the training in quality tools may improve on-time delivery performance, which may improve customer satisfaction and therefore increase return on investment. At some companies, the connection between customer satisfaction and return on investment is based on the observation that more satisfied customers pay invoices faster, which results in increased accounts receivable turnover, which increases return on investment.

Chapter 4

Guidelines for Using Balanced Scorecards to Manage and Measure Performance

Performance measures that are highly aligned with and linked to an organization's business strategy are critical for communicating and executing strategy.[1] Here are some guidelines for using Balanced Scorecards to measure and manage strategy.

1. Remember, strategy and performance measures are inseparable.

At many organizations, there are serious gaps between strategy and performance measures. This is often the result of the separation between strategy development processes and performance measurement (strategy execution) processes. Instead, organizations should treat strategy development and strategy execution as parallel, interrelated processes. Strategy-focused performance measures are driven by a process that encompasses the ongoing reevaluation and redesign of business strategy, and ensures that strategy execution through performance measurement is part and parcel of the strategy design itself. This approach leads naturally to the types of performance measures the Balanced Scorecard and other strategic performance measurement systems encourage.

2. Always begin with strategy.

Ignoring this guideline is a common problem. The first question some managers ask when embarking on a performance measurement initiative is, "What should we measure?" or "How should we measure performance in a given area?" or "How many performance measures should we have in our scorecard?" In fact, any of these questions is the last thing management should focus on. Strategic performance measurement systems, such as the Balanced Scorecard, are first and foremost about strategy. This requires the development of a business strategy with execution in mind. Once the strategy is well developed, performance metrics can be identified.

3. Align strategy and performance measures with the right goal.

The highest tenet of business strategy is to ethically manage for the creation of maximum financial value. This goal provides the anchor that will help management make the right decisions in developing and executing the business strategy. Strategic performance measures must be focused on maximizing financial value creation, although many companies fail to do this because of misaligned compensation plans and/or misdirected motivations. As recent events have dramatically shown, the use of stock options can have quite the problematic incentive effects. Are the performance measures used in your organization truly leading to managing for maximum financial value creation? Or are flawed financial metrics leading in the wrong direction? Increases in revenues and earnings per share (EPS) are still widely reported as primary metrics of determining value creation. When business decisions are based on those metrics, however, the results can be disastrous, such as value-destroying mergers and acquisitions, growth at the expense of return on investment, and harvesting of assets, which may increase accounting profits, but actually destroy value.

4. Metrics should change as strategy changes.

Too often, organizations use performance measures that are no longer relevant to their business strategy. Existing strategy can become outdated because products and services are less needed by the marketplace, the market segment may be shrinking in size, or the way the organization creates or delivers the product or service offerings may become outmoded as new technologies become available or laws and regulations restrict or allow activities to change. It is critical that organizations consider how forces of change affect the entire value chain and how those changes can affect the interrelationships of accompanying activities. All of this affects performance measures.

During the late 1990s, technology took center stage, reshaping the way companies conduct business and the demands consumers place on the goods and services they receive, as companies like Dell have proven. Dell's initial strategy and performance metrics differed from competitors like Compaq. Dell initially focused on operating effectively and efficiently, which, in part, involved shortening its cash conversion cycle by managing days' sales outstanding, days in inventory, and days' payables outstanding. But when the market demanded more innovation of offerings in product and post-sales service, Dell needed to adjust its strategy and performance metrics accordingly.

5. Use performance measures that help synchronize strategic activities.

How well do existing performance measures enable your organization to synchronize the combination of strategic competencies and supporting activities to fulfill customer needs in large, growing market segments? In successful companies, all strategic activities are closely aligned and synchronized to create the right kinds of offerings.

Strategic performance measures should be closely focused and driven from the strategy. Michael Porter of Harvard Business School puts it this way, "Measure how various parts of your value chain actually fit together to lead to an overarching advantage, rather than using process-by-process metrics."[2] Are your performance measures truly unique and relevant to the strategy of the organization?

These guidelines can provide an alternative to the endless performance metric debates that have plagued corporate management over the past decade. Strategic performance measurement begins with a sound philosophy pertaining to, and a sound judgment surrounding, how strategic decisions will be made and how performance measurement will be used to make decisions and execute the strategy. Management must be vigilant in aligning performance measures with the strategy of the organization and in ensuring the strategy is executable and viable.

The Six-Stage Management System

The six-stage strategy execution system developed by Kaplan and Norton provides an excellent perspective on how performance measures and results are used in executing and refining strategy.[3]

1. **Develop the strategy.** Establish the organization's mission, vision, and strategy.

2. **Translate the strategy.** Include the strategy in Strategy Maps and Balanced Scorecard performance measures.

3. **Align the organization.** Align organizational units through the use of the Balanced Scorecard.

4. **Plan operations.** Develop operational plans and budgets.

5. **Monitor and learn.** Use strategy reviews and operational reviews to learn and refine the strategy and its execution.

6. **Test and adapt.** Set the stage for strategy refinement and development.

This six-stage management system (most importantly, stages 1 and 2) can be adapted in developing Balanced Scorecards and Strategy Maps for internal audit departments.

Departmental Scorecards

When developing performance measures, department heads should consider key strategy-related questions:

- How aligned are departmental performance measures to departmental and corporate strategies?

- How well does the departmental budget link to departmental and corporate strategies?

- How should we prioritize strategic initiatives?

- How well are individuals/teams in the department aligned to strategy?

Summary

The last two chapters presented an overview of the Balanced Scorecard and Strategy Maps to provide perspective on the way organizations manage and measure performance. In the next two chapters, I describe strategy frameworks for developing a strategy and strategic objectives for an internal audit function, which is the first step for developing a Balanced Scorecard for internal audit.

Chapter 5
Return Driven Strategy Framework

Prior to developing a Balanced Scorecard and Strategy Map for an internal audit function, the strategy and strategic objectives must be defined before the accompanying performance measures can be developed in a Balanced Scorecard. The next three chapters describe the Return Driven Strategy framework (introduced in the 2002 report) and the Mission Driven Strategy framework, and the importance of building a strategic internal audit function with a business perspective.[1] I also discuss the importance of linking internal audit strategy with the strategy of the enterprise, and introduce the strategic governance, risk, and compliance (GRC) framework to help CAEs develop strategic objectives that relate to risk assessment and risk management.[2]

The Return Driven Strategy framework is a way to think about internal audit as a business and to help connect its strategy with that of the enterprise. It can help CAEs to understand the enterprise's strategy and develop a relevant strategy for internal audit. It describes the pattern of strategic activities of high-performance companies, regardless of industry or geographic location, and includes the strategic activities of high-performance companies, as described in the book, *DRIVEN: Business Strategy, Humans Actions, and the Creation of Wealth.*[3]

The Return Driven Strategy framework is based on extensive research of the financial performance data of more than 20,000 companies for more than 30 years of data, along with detailed study of the pattern of strategic activities in those that met stringent criteria for sustainable high performance. These companies showed superior performance for ten consecutive years or more in three key performance measures: return on investment (ROI), growth, and total shareholder returns. Cash flow ROI was at least twice that of the corporate average for at least ten consecutive years, growth rates in investments made in the business exceeded average market growth, and total shareholder returns outperformed the market for at least a ten-year period. Approximately 100 Return Driven companies that are currently publicly traded met this set of criteria.

The Return Driven Strategy framework includes 11 tenets that represent the path to ethically create wealth. (The tenets are shown in the 11 rectangular boxes in **figure 5.1**.[4]) Tenets are arranged in a pyramid from top to bottom in order of impact on long-term financial results and valuations.

Each level in the pyramid represents a type of tenet. These levels are:

- Commitment tenet
- Goal tenets
- Competency tenets
- Supporting tenets

Finally, the pyramid rests on three foundations, which summarize key factors of business strategy that apply to each of the 11 tenets. These foundations are (1) genuine assets, (2) vigilance to forces of change, and (3) disciplined performance measure and valuation.

Commitment Tenet

1. Ethically Maximize Wealth

The first tenet, which appears at the top of the Return Driven Strategy pyramid, focuses on the commitment of companies to create the most value with their resources and to do so within the ethical parameters of their constituents and communities.

More important than any other tenet, management must:

- Be committed and focused on maximizing shareholder value (achieving long-term and sustainable ROI) as its primary objective

- Manage the drivers of wealth creation—ROI and strategic growth

- *Always* function within the ethical boundaries and parameters set by its constituents and the communities in which the business operates (or hopes to operate in the future)

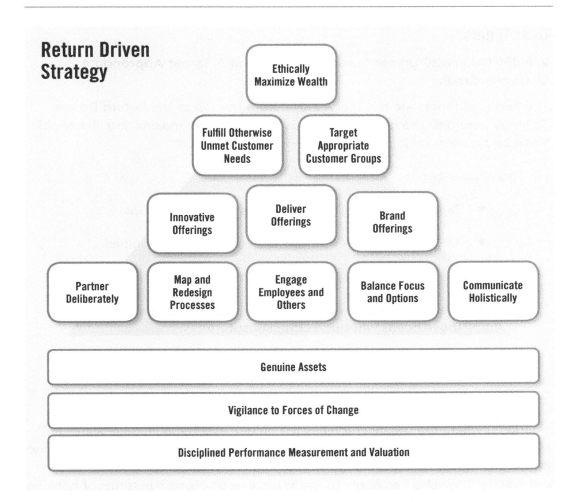

Figure 5.1. Return Driven Strategy Framework

Version 7.2 Copyright ©2000-2007, Mark L. Frigo and Joel Litman. Used with permission.

Described by Kathy Apple, CEO of the National Council of State Boards of Nursing (NCSBN) as "doing the right things for the right reasons," this tenet also includes the controls and governance necessary to conduct business within the ethical parameters of constituents and communities. Internal auditors provide a valuable resource for supporting this tenet of strategy.

Goal Tenets

2. Fulfill Otherwise Unmet Customer Needs and 3. Target Appropriate Customer Groups

The two goal tenets are the second level from the top of the Return Driven Strategy pyramid. The goal tenets focus on the path to maximizing shareholder value by creating value for customers—lots of customers.

This is done by:

- Targeting *economically* profitable customer groups
- Targeting customer groups with growth opportunities
- Identifying *otherwise unmet needs* of customers
- Creating (innovating) and delivering offerings that fulfill those needs without a close substitute
- Being the dominant fulfiller of that customer group's needs

The goal tenets focus attention on customer needs and customer groups (markets) where the organization has the unique and valuable capabilities and resources, or genuine assets. These tenets can help internal auditors understand how the business creates value for its customers, which, in turn, drives financial results. They also can apply to the internal audit process in terms of fulfilling otherwise unmet customer needs and serving the right customer groups.

Competency Tenets

4. Deliver Offerings, 5. Innovate Offerings, and 6. Brand Offerings

The competency tenets, which are the third level from the top of the pyramid, focus on the *offerings* that the organization provides for the customer. The business must effectively deliver *need-answering* offerings, while balancing convenience and cost to the customer. Given scarce resources of time and money, a customer's needs are never really fulfilled—meanwhile, profitable offerings quickly attract substitutes. Therefore, *continuous* innovation (changing) of offerings) is necessary. Finally, the consumer's mind must be branded with an indelible connection between an explicit understanding of need and the offering that uniquely fulfills it. Branding is defined as making the connection between your offering and the customer's unmet need in the mind and heart of the customer. The *executability* of plans must be tackled at the outset of strategy evaluation.

The competency tenets help internal auditors understand how internal processes drive customer performance, which, in turn, drives financial performance. Internal auditors can think about their own competency tenets in terms of how well they innovate, deliver, and brand their offerings.

Supporting Tenets

7. – 11. Activities to Better Achieve the Higher Tenets of the Pyramid

Five overlapping groups of activities (tenets 7-11) serve to enhance a business's strategy and execution (see **figure 5.1**, the third level from the top of the pyramid). They include:

7. Partner deliberately
8. Map and redesign processes
9. Engage employees and others
10. Balance focus and options
11. Communicate holistically

Great performance is evident when these activities are focused on driving innovation, operational superiority, and branding in order to achieve the goal tenets and maximize shareholder wealth. Poor performance follows firms that engage in these supporting tenets indiscriminately.

The supporting tenets can help internal auditors understand the strategic activities that support the competency tenets and the role the internal audit function plays in these activities. The internal auditors also can think about the supporting tenets in terms of partnering deliberately with internal and external partners, understanding and improving the internal audit value chain, balancing the focus on current internal audit activities while considering innovation and growth options, communicating holistically to ensure internal audit effectiveness, and developing the internal audit brand.

Three Foundations of Business Strategy

As shown in **figure 5.1,** the three foundations of business strategy are (1) genuine assets, (2) vigilance to forces of change, and (3) disciplined performance measure and valuation. The following section explains these foundations and the questions that CAEs should ask about them.

1. Genuine Assets

As the 11 tenets are the *verbs* of strategy, the genuine assets are the nouns. Over time, activities are copied by competitors and followed by price competition, and returns are reduced. By leveraging un-copiable assets (which are assets that cannot be copied, such as proprietary customer information, unique capabilities, patents, leading economies of scale and scope, distribution chain monopolies, etc.), a business can create un-substitutable offerings (offerings for which the customer cannot find a substitute). With that comes the potential for pricing premiums, higher margins and/or asset efficiency, and above-average returns and valuation. Coupled with activities described in the 11 tenets, genuine assets are the building blocks of a sustainable competitive advantage.

Questions CAEs Should Ask about the Organization's Genuine Assets

- What are the most important genuine assets of the organization?
- How are they leveraged in the strategy?
- What are the missing genuine assets that would allow the organization to create more value?
- Which genuine assets are at risk and how can they be protected?
- What role does internal audit play in protecting the organization's genuine assets?

Return Driven Strategy Framework

Questions CAEs Should Ask about the Internal Audit Function's Genuine Assets

- What are the most important genuine assets of internal audit?
- How are they leveraged in the internal audit function's strategy?
- What are the missing genuine assets that would allow the function to create more value?

2. Vigilance to Forces of Change

The Greek letter and symbol for change in mathematics (delta, Δ) forms the backdrop of the pyramid. Because business environments are so dynamic, management must leverage opportunities and avoid or manage threats arising in pursuit of each of the tenets. Major areas for vigilance include:

- Government, legal, and regulatory change
- Demographic and cultural shifts and trends
- Scientific and technological breakthroughs
- Industry and competition

This foundation relates to the risks and opportunities in forces of change.

Questions CAEs Should Ask about the Organization's Vigilance to Forces of Change

- What forces of change will create the most risk for the organization?
- What forces of change will create the most opportunities for the organization?

Questions CAEs Should Ask about the Internal Audit Function's Vigilance to Forces of Change

- What forces of change will create the most risk for internal audit?

- What forces of change will create the most opportunities for internal audit?

3. Disciplined Performance Measurement and Valuation

This is the bedrock foundation of the framework. Performance measures must be aligned with the tenets and foundations of the Return Driven Strategy. Performance measures should also be highly aligned with superior long-term ROI. And performance measures should include some key risk indicators for effective strategic risk management.

Questions CAEs Should Ask About Disciplined Performance Measurement and Valuation

- Does the organization have the right metrics that are aligned with long-term wealth creation?

- Does the internal audit function have the right metrics that reflect its strategic vision and value?

Thinking of Internal Audit as a Business

One way to develop a strategic internal audit function is to use the Return Driven Strategy framework in thinking of internal audit as a business. For example, tenet 2 of the Return Driven Strategy framework, which focuses on identifying and fulfilling a customer's unmet needs, can help CAEs develop a strategy that, first and foremost, addresses stakeholder needs. Tenet 3 (targeting and serving appropriate customer groups) can help CAEs develop a strategy to identify new stakeholder groups and create additional value. Tenet 5, which refers to fulfilling otherwise unmet needs, can help CAEs develop a strategy driven by changing customer needs. Strategic partnering (tenet 7) suggests including internal and external partnering as part of the internal audit strategy. CAEs can identify genuine assets and how they are (or could be) leveraged in the strategy of an internal audit function. The framework's disciplined performance measurement and valuation can serve as the foundation for developing strategic internal audit objectives and performance measures for an internal audit Balanced Scorecard.

Balanced Scorecard and Strategy Map Integration

The architecture of the Return Driven Strategy is consistent with that of the Balanced Scorecard. The Balanced Scorecard architecture comprises financial, customer, internal processes, and innovation and growth perspectives.

Tenet 1 of the Return Driven Strategy framework (to ethically create wealth) represents the financial perspective of the Balanced Scorecard architecture. Tenets 2 and 3 (to fulfill otherwise unmet needs and target appropriate customer groups) represent the customer perspective. The competency tenets (4, 5, and 6) and the supporting tenets represent the internal processes perspective and the innovation and growth perspective. The genuine assets, which are unique (tangible and intangible) resources and capabilities, fall under the Balanced Scorecard's innovation and growth perspective. Vigilance to forces of change is relevant to monitoring economic factors, technological factors, social factors, and laws and regulations, which also drive innovation and growth. Disciplined performance measures and valuation naturally fit well within the Balanced Scorecard approach.

Insight from Internal Audit Leaders

The following question-and-answer features provide insight and perspective for applying the Return Driven Strategy framework to an internal audit function. Dick Anderson, clinical professor of strategic risk management at DePaul University, discusses how key tenets of the framework help CAEs and internal auditors to develop a strategy by thinking of internal audit as a business. Paul Walker, from St. John's University School of Risk Management, discusses keys to success for developing a strategic internal audit function.

Thinking of Internal Audit as a Business

Richard J. (Dick) Anderson, Partner (retired) PricewaterhouseCoopers LLP, Clinical Professor of Strategic Risk Management, DePaul University

Note: Although the entire Return Driven Strategy framework can be used to develop an internal audit strategy, Dick Anderson focuses here on the aspects he believes are most critical for the internal audit function.

Focus on Internal Audit Customer Needs (Tenet 2)

My experience is that this tenet is the key to both internal audit's strategy and how the function will add value to the organization. Explicitly understanding and then exceeding the expectations of key stakeholders is how internal audit becomes viewed as a value-adding function. While internal audit can have multiple stakeholders, the audit committee and executive management are the drivers and their expectations are the ones that matter most. At PwC, we referred to these expectations as "value drivers," as they are the stakeholder's proxy for the value they expect from internal audit. Internal audit must explicitly understand these expectations and also validate them back to the stakeholders to ensure that there is clarity and agreement.

Deliver Offerings (Tenet 4)

Internal audit needs to follow the example of many of its businesses and seek the most efficient and effective operating processes. It must constantly challenge itself to be highly effective in its operations and consider how to improve and innovate delivery of its services. This can entail activities such as reviews and comparisons with leading practices and the deployment of new audit approaches and tools. Similar to most businesses, technology offers significant opportunities to improve both efficiency and effectiveness of audit operations.

Strategic Partnering (Tenet 7)

One of the valuable lessons learned during the financial crisis was the need for organizations to move away from "siloed" risk and control units to increase the amount of collaboration and information sharing. This is especially the case with the organization's risks. Accordingly, internal audit needs to consider how effectively they partner with their related risk and control functions as a core part of their strategy. This is not an organizational structure or reporting line issue, but rather a mindset issue. All the risk and control functions are serving and protecting the same organization and, therefore, need to be open to information sharing and seeking opportunities for better collaboration. This partnering and sharing can be done without any impairment of internal audit independence.

Engage Employees and Others (Tenet 9)

Few, if any, internal audit functions have all the skills and knowledge that they need to keep up with today's fast-paced environment. Therefore, internal audit's strategy should consider what skills it needs to address the risk profile of the organization, which of these skills it has or can reasonably develop, and which it might need from third-party support.

Vigilant to the Forces of Change (Foundation 2)

Probably the greatest challenge facing most internal audit organizations today is understanding and keeping up with changing risks. Internal audit must then challenge its own processes for risk assessment, risk monitoring, and risk identification. This must include both the internal risks related to the strategy of its business and the external and systemic risks that could impact the organization's ability to meet its business objectives. Accordingly, a CAE must have a strategic view of the organization and its businesses and be attuned to changes—both internal and external—and then ensure that the audit coverage is appropriately revised to keep pace with those changes.

Disciplined Performance Measurement and Valuation (Foundation 3)

The best advice I can give a CAE is to ensure that performance measures clearly align with and address the expectations of the key stakeholders, and then to periodically report on performance related to each of those expectations. Too often, I observed internal audit functions diligently tracking and reporting on internally focused performance measures that, unfortunately, did not reflect or measure performance against the specific expectations of their key stakeholders. That misalignment is a recipe for disaster.

Developing a Strategic Internal Audit Function

Dr. Paul L. Walker, James J. Schiro/Zurich Chair in Enterprise Risk Management at St. John's University, Center for Excellence in ERM at St. John's School of Risk Management

How would you describe the keys to success for developing a strategic internal audit function and becoming a more strategic internal auditor?

Internal auditors have to learn to think differently. That means understanding the business, the strategy, and the related risks. It will require that they adopt a different view of the company—a view that may stretch their thinking way beyond auditing. My study describes several CAEs that have altered their thinking and become more strategic.

One of the themes of this book is "Developing a Strategy for an Internal Audit Function," which includes "The Importance of Linking Internal Audit Strategy with the Strategy of the Enterprise." Based on your research, what are some of the keys to success for doing this?

Our study shows the key is to first understand the business and then to take the initiative and get involved. In some cases, you've got to be ready to show you've got skills that are valuable to the board and C-suite.

What advice would you give CAEs to help them develop strategic internal audit functions?

After changing their thinking about how they can contribute, auditors may need more training. This can include business acumen, business modeling, strategy, and enterprise risk management. Additional training and skills may be critical thinking, consulting, listening, and facilitation.

Chapter 6
Mission Driven Strategy Framework

"Mission drift" is a challenge for nonprofit organizations, as well as departmental units in companies. The Mission Driven Strategy framework[1] is designed to help leaders better focus and align activities and resources with the intentions and mission of the organization. The framework helps an organization determine whether it is doing the right things for the right reasons. Recently, a CEO of a large nonprofit commented, "The value of Mission Driven Strategy has consistently rung true for me as it has helped us focus on the right initiatives and objectives for the right reasons to best serve the organization."

As depicted in **figure 6.1**, the Mission Driven Strategy can help CAEs to develop, refine, and align a strategy for Fulfilling Otherwise Unmet Constituent (Stakeholder) Needs and Serving the Right Constituents.

The Commitment Tenet

1. Ethically Maximize Mission-Based Value

In Mission Driven Strategy, the highest tenet is commit to ethically maximize mission-based value. This tenet describes the disciplined commitment to create value as defined by an organization's mission, and to do so ethically. It means having the right objectives, performance measures, and structure to be able to create and maximize mission-based value. In other words, Mission Driven Strategy can help CAEs answer the question, "Are we doing the right things for the right reasons?"

The Balanced Scorecard

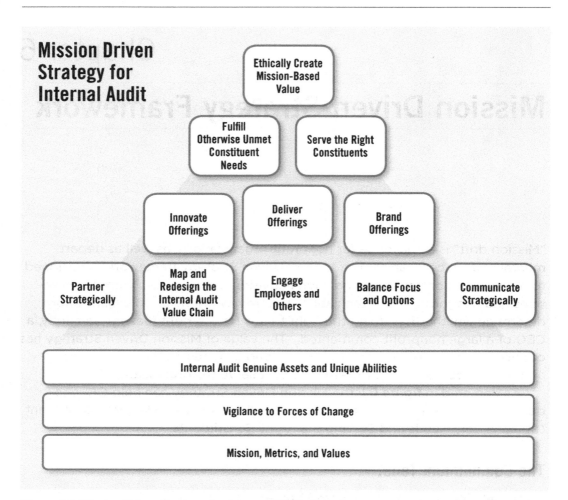

Figure 6.1. Mission Driven Strategy for Internal Audit

Version 1.0 Adapted from Return Driven Strategy-Frigo & Litman. ©Copyright 2013 Dr. Mark L. Frigo. Used with permission.

The Goal Tenets

2. Fulfill Constituents' Otherwise Unmet Needs and 3. Target the Right Constituents

The two goal tenets of a Mission Driven Strategy help internal auditors to keep the needs of targeted constituent segments in sight, as well as to target the right segments. The internal audit function can more directly fulfill these needs when they are well defined. One would question the validity of a mission that targets a shrinking base of needs, particularly if the needs are being met elsewhere.

The Competency Tenets

4. Deliver Offerings, 5. Innovate Offerings, and 6. Brand Offerings

The ability to execute plans must be tackled at the outset of strategy evaluation. The organization must effectively deliver need-answering offerings and balance convenience and cost to its constituents. Given scarce resources, a constituent's needs are never really fulfilled. Meanwhile, new offerings quickly attract substitutes. Therefore, continuous innovation of offerings is necessary. Finally, the constituents' mind must be branded with an indelible connection between an explicit need and the offering that will uniquely fulfill it.

The Supporting Tenets

7. – 11. Activities to Better Achieve the Higher Tenets of the Pyramid

The five overlapping groups of activities that serve to enhance internal audit strategy and execution include:

- Partnering strategically
- Mapping and redesigning processes
- Engaging employees and others
- Balancing focus and options
- Communicating strategically

Great performance is evident when these activities focus on driving innovation, operational superiority, and branding to achieve the goal tenets and maximize the value of mission-based strategy. Poor performance follows organizations that indiscriminately engage in these supporting tenets, without focusing on the goal tenets of mission-based strategy.

Foundations

Genuine Assets, Forces of Change, Performance Measurement

Coupled with activities described in the 11 tenets, genuine assets are the building blocks of creating value.

There are three major areas for vigilance: 1) government, legal, and other regulatory change, 2) demographic and cultural shifts, and 3) scientific and technological breakthroughs. Vigilance is required for internal audit to stay abreast of the risks and opportunities in these forces of change.

Certain performance measurement guidelines are necessary for effective strategy execution. Performance measures used in the organization must be aligned with the tenets of a Mission Driven Strategy to be successful. Organizations with performance measures that are not well aligned with the tenets of Mission Driven Strategy may focus on the wrong activities, rather than "doing the right things for the right reasons." The Balanced Scorecard and its underlying principles provide a suitable framework for performance measurement in internal audit functions.

Strategic Vision and Strategic Intent of Internal Audit

The concept of strategic intent, introduced by Gary Hamel and C. K. Prahalad,[2] is relevant as a way to think about developing a strategic vision for the internal audit function. Every CAE should consider what the function might need to do differently.

CAEs can use the Return Driven Strategy framework and Mission Driven Strategy framework to help develop the function's strategic intent and strategic vision. Helpful questions to be addressed include:

- What otherwise unmet customer and constituent needs does internal audit fulfill in the organization?

- How are those needs changing?

- How well is internal audit innovating its offerings to better fulfill customer/constituent needs?

- How well is internal audit innovating its offerings to fulfill the changing needs of its constituents?

- What is the brand of internal audit? (What are three words that others would use to describe internal audit? What three words would you like your constituents use to describe internal audit?)

The Stop-Doing List

Another way to think about developing a strategic vision for internal audit is to develop a "disciplined" strategy that not only identifies what internal audit should be doing, but also identifies the things it should stop doing. This philosophy is consistent with the work of Jim Collins in his best-selling book, *Good to Great*, which suggests that the key steps that drive transformation of companies from good to great are not only what they do, but what they stop doing. One of the most famous cases was Kimberly-Clark, which decided to sell off its paper mills and focus on its consumer products business (such as Kleenex®).[3]

Jim Collins discusses the idea of a "stop-doing list," which provides great insight on developing a focused strategy to create more value.[4] The Return Driven Strategy framework and Mission Driven Strategy framework can help CAEs create a more valuable and focused strategic vision and determine which activities they should stop doing.

The Importance of a Well-Defined Strategy for Internal Audit

A clear and well-defined strategy is the first step for developing a Balanced Scorecard for internal audit. Larry Harrington, vice president–internal audit at Raytheon Company, explains the necessity of a well-defined internal audit strategy to create value and achieve success:

> Without a well-defined strategy, CAEs will struggle or even fail to establish the proper priorities, and then to allocate resources that align to what key stakeholders expect and value from their internal audit function.

Insight for Internal Audit Leaders

The following question-and-answer feature provides insight on the importance of linking the strategy of internal audit with the strategy of the enterprise, which sets the stage for developing a Balanced Scorecard for internal audit. Kathy Swain, senior vice president of internal audit at Allstate Insurance, discusses the importance of linking internal audit strategy with the enterprise strategy.

Linking Internal Audit Strategy with the Strategy of the Enterprise

Kathy Swain, Senior Vice President of Internal Audit, Allstate Insurance

Why is it important for internal audit's strategy to be linked to the strategy of the enterprise?

Unlike our external or regulatory audit colleagues, an internal audit department will not be successful unless its organization is successful. Balancing this, along with the expectations of other constituents (shareholders, regulators, professional expectations, etc.), is one of the key challenges of an internal auditor's job.

Our job doesn't end with the articulation of an opinion on the state of the internal controls. We need to ensure that our audits provide the business with real assurance that the risks to achieving business objectives have been appropriately mitigated. If they are not, we need to help them understand what controls would assist them in mitigating the risk. As risks change, we must learn and adapt our audit practices. We need to simultaneously be professional practitioners and change agents.

What advice would you give to CAEs to help them ensure this linkage?

Work hard to get the transparency to the business. Once you have it, and you understand where the business is headed, think about the implications of change to the existing control environment. Consider what changes are needed to the internal audit department's people (capabilities and skills), processes, and technology to understand the risks, evaluate controls, and influence improvements. Map out the steps that you need to take to achieve these changes. Bring your team along with you on this journey so that, once an internal audit strategy is agreed, they understand what it is and why things need to change.

What advice would you give to CAEs in developing internal audit scorecard performance measures that are linked to the strategy of the enterprise?

I would advise them to visualize that both the business and the internal audit function have successfully implemented their strategies and that they are getting what is expected from the investment made in the change. I would ask them to think about what is different; how much more timely or effective audits are now, how satisfied stakeholders are, the different skills and abilities that are now available to deploy... Then I would suggest that they think about how they would evidence this. That is the data that they should design and capture to track progress to achieving these goals.

Chapter 7

A Strategic GRC Framework

The strategy of an internal audit function may include activities related to governance, risk, and compliance (GRC). A source of some confusion and misunderstanding related to GRC has been the lack of a basic conceptual model or framework. To address this problem, I present a strategic GRC framework. The framework has three basic components:

- A strategically focused top section tied into ultimate shareholder value

- A middle section representing the individual GRC functions (including internal audit)

- A bottom section comprising common, integrated processes

The strategic GRC framework, as shown in **figure 7.1**, can be used by internal auditors to develop a strategy for GRC initiatives.[1]

The top strategic section and, in particular, the board-level risk policy segment represent a key element of the framework. It requires a common view of organizational value creation and protection and provides a set of shared, high-level risk policies to ensure consistency of purpose, view, and thinking across GRC functions. This top-down approach also drives greater communication among GRC functions and more consistent reporting. Bottom-up approaches, by contrast, can easily fail, as they increase the likelihood that units operating in a silo may continue to pursue their own goals and objectives in the absence of a policy from the top. Without this strategic umbrella in place, achieving GRC benefits can be very difficult.

The Balanced Scorecard

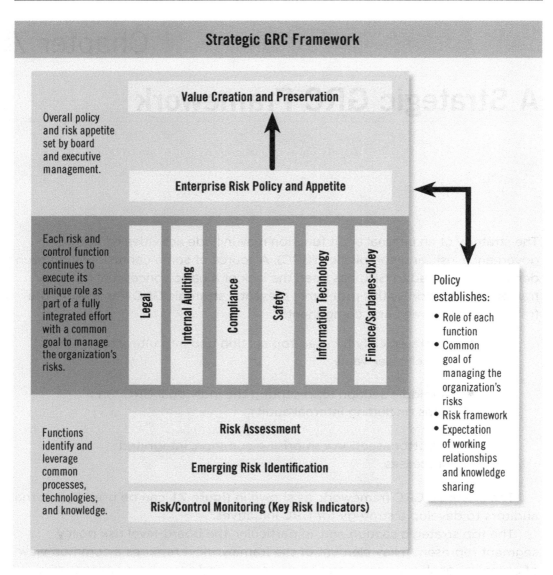

Figure 7.1. Strategic GRC Framework

©Copyright 2009 by Mark L. Frigo and Richard J. Anderson.

Source: Frigo and Anderson, "Strategic GRC: 10 Steps to Implementation," *Internal Auditor* (June 2009). Used with permission.

The middle portion of the framework recognizes that individual functions have unique roles that must be maintained for the integrity of organizational governance. This component is especially relevant for internal audit. Without a clear acknowledgment of each function's value, organizations simply looking to cut costs may be tempted to distort internal audit's role or merge it with other GRC functions.

The framework's bottom section identifies core processes that can be leveraged across GRC functions. It also emphasizes that, once the strategic framework is in place and understood, the organization should consider whether future investments in knowledge capabilities and technology can be made on a collaborative basis.

The GRC framework can be a useful tool for internal auditors seeking both to foster understanding and facilitate implementation of GRC initiatives. Internal auditors and their clients should keep in mind, however, that while the framework helps organizations think and act with high-level consistency, it is not meant to serve as a restructured organizational chart.

For more information about implementing the strategic GRC framework, see the article by Mark L. Frigo and Richard J. Anderson, "10 Steps to Implement the Strategic GRC Framework" *Internal Auditor* (June 2009). The 10-step approach is intended to provide a platform for learning, education, and buy-in. For further reading on the strategic GRC framework and its role in strategic risk management, see the book by Mark L. Frigo and Richard J. Anderson, *Strategic Risk Management: A Primer for Directors and Management Teams,* 2010.

Chapter 8

Developing a Balanced Scorecard for the Internal Audit Function

Applying the Balanced Scorecard framework to internal audit is based on the premise that key performance measures can help CAEs execute departmental strategy and communicate that strategy. The Balanced Scorecard can help them to focus internal audit activities on value-added services and corporate strategies and priorities. The challenge is developing and using performance measures that are consistent with departmental strategy and relevant to different customer groups, changing customer priorities, and changing environment.

An approach for using a Balanced Scorecard framework for the internal audit function is based on the following assumptions:

- Performance metrics should be driven by the internal audit function's mission and strategy, as well as the strategy of the enterprise.

- Performance metrics should include customer measures, internal process measures, and capability and innovation measures.

- Performance metrics for internal audit functions should include leading indicators (performance drivers), as well as lagging indicators (outcome measures).

A Balanced Scorecard for internal audit functions can be based on the following three steps:

1. Develop the strategy for the internal audit function.

2. Use the concept of Strategy Maps to understand the interrelationship among strategic objectives in the strategy.

3. Develop performance measures for the Balanced Scorecard, along with targets and action plans.

The architecture for a Balanced Scorecard for an internal audit department can be adapted to meet the needs of the organization and department, including customer perspective(s), internal process perspective, innovation, and capabilities perspective.

One internal audit department that I studied noticed it was missing the mark on improving controls and finding cost improvement opportunities, so it used its Balance Scorecard metrics and linkages to focus its activities on the key customer metrics in those areas.

One reason for developing a Balanced Scorecard framework for internal audit is that departmental performance measures can be improved by applying the principles of the Balanced Scorecard. In assessing the performance measures of a department, like internal audit, the following questions should be addressed:

- Do departmental performance measures reflect the department's mission statement?

- Do departmental performance measures reflect corporate strategy and initiatives?

- Do performance measures include performance drivers (leading indicators), as well as outcome measures (lagging indicators)?

- Do performance measures reflect the departmental value proposition?

- Are linkages among different performance measures understood and managed?

- Do performance measures reflect your unique strategic role within the organization?

The Balanced Scorecard is first and foremost about strategy. Therefore, accompanying performance measures are logically derived from strategy. The execution of strategy is improved by developing Strategy Maps, which show a clear cause-and-effect linkage among strategic objectives and performance measures. An issue intimately related to performance measures is the assessment of department strategy. According to Michael Porter, strategy is the "creation of a unique and valuable position, involving a different set of activities."[1] Before performance measures can be assessed and improved, the strategy of the department needs to be assessed and refined.

The tenets of Return Driven Strategy and Mission Driven Strategy can be used by CAEs in reviewing and refining their strategy for internal audit, which sets the stage for development of the Balanced Scorecard. How does the department fulfill unmet needs within the organization? How will the department innovate its offerings? How does it engage its employees?

The Balanced Scorecard can help internal audit functions to be agile in terms of the changes in the environment and organization. Larry Harrington, vice president–internal audit at Raytheon Company, explained:

> Tools such as Balanced Scorecards and Strategy Maps enhance the CAE's ability to manage and measure department effectiveness and efficiency, especially in today's environment where the internal audit mandate can shift abruptly to organizational and environmental changes.

Developing an Architecture for an Internal Audit Scorecard

Adapting the Balanced Scorecard framework to internal audit requires identification of performance measurement categories. As shown in **figure 8.1**, the following four perspectives are proposed:

- Board/audit committee
- Management and audit customers (clients)
- Internal audit processes
- Learning, innovation, and capabilities of internal audit[2]

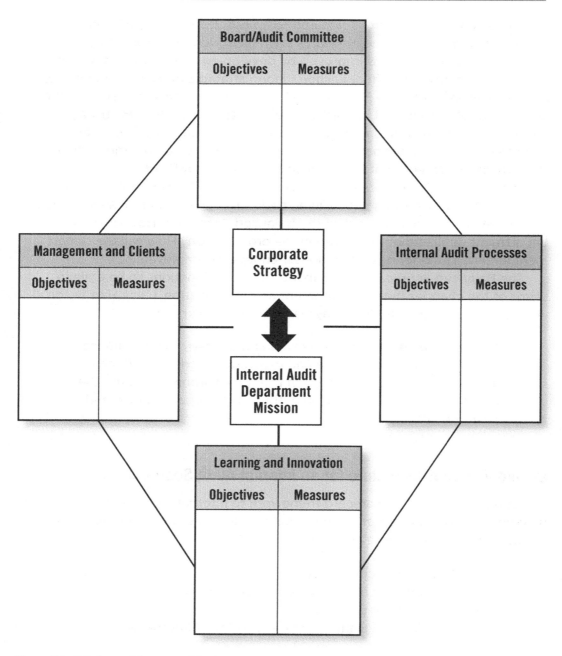

Figure 8.1. A Balanced Scorecard for Internal Audit

Author's creation.

The first two perspectives of the scorecard focus on the two primary customer groups of internal audit: board/audit committee and management/audit customers. Internal audit processes represent a third perspective. Finally, innovation and capabilities of internal audit refer to staff, technology, and training.

Corporate strategy and internal audit department strategy are the fundamental drivers of the Balanced Scorecard for internal audit. Both will have some impact on the strategic objectives of the internal audit department. In turn, these strategic objectives will determine the primary strategic performance measures used in the Balanced Scorecard.

Examples of Strategic Objectives and Performance Measures in a Scorecard

One way to show overall examples of a Balanced Scorecard for internal audit is to delineate strategic objectives and related performance measures under the four categories used in this study.

Board/Audit Committee Perspective

Strategic Objective	Performance Measure
Improve audit committee satisfaction.	Audit committee satisfaction survey score
Establish internal audit as a key audit committee resource of internal control expertise.	Role of internal audit as viewed by the audit committee through audit committee survey questions

The overall strategic objective of these performance measures is to "improve the internal audit department's standing with the audit committee." Improving audit committee satisfaction can be measured with a satisfaction survey score, which can be linked to more specific survey questions about the performance of the internal audit department. Wanting to establish itself as a valuable resource for internal control expertise, the internal audit department can obtain information on perceptions and measure progress by formulating relevant questions for surveying the audit committee.

Management/Audit Customer Perspective

Strategic Objective	Performance Measure
Improve level of audit customer satisfaction.	Audit customer satisfaction survey score
Decrease number of complaints about the audit department.	Number of complaints about audit department
Increase percentage of audit recommendations implemented.	Percent of audit recommendations implemented
Increase number of management requests for audit services.	Number of management requests

The overall theme of these strategic objectives and performance measures is to improve management and audit customer satisfaction and internal audit's role within the organization. This involves direct measures of audit customer and management satisfaction, as well as indirect measures, such as the percentage of audit recommendations implemented and the requests for audit services. It also includes inverse measures of performance, such as reducing the number of complaints about the audit department.

Internal Audit Processes Perspective

Strategic Objective	Performance Measure
Implement departmental process improvements.	Number of departmental process improvements
Increase ratio of completed to planned audits.	Number of completed vs. planned audits
Increase number of audit finding recommendations.	Number of major audit finding recommendations
Decrease fieldwork time for audits.	Days from end of fieldwork to report issuance

Here we see strategic objectives and performance measures focusing on process improvement, effectiveness in completing audits, productivity in terms of audit finding, and efficiency in fieldwork.

Innovation and Capabilities Perspective

Strategic Objective	Performance Measure
Develop and retain an experienced audit department.	Years of staff experience and average years of audit experience
Develop and retain a department with high levels of education credentials and certifications.	Number of staff with advance degrees and percent of certified staff
Maintain continuing professional education for the internal audit department.	Training hours per internal auditor

Here we see a variety of strategic objectives and performance measures aimed at the capabilities of the department that support the function's internal processes and, in turn, drive customer performance.

Strategy Maps help managers focus on a strategic theme and link strategic objectives and performance measures in a cause-and-effect chain, such as to "Improve customer satisfaction through providing value-added services" and "Improve productivity and responsiveness."

The cause-and-effect chain on the continuum can be described as a series of *if/then* statements. *If* training hours per internal auditor are increased, *then* the number of process improvements will increase. *If* the number of process improvements increases, *then* the percentage of audit recommendations implemented will increase. *If* the percentage of audit recommendations implemented increases, *then* audit customer satisfaction will increase. Notice that although "number of process improvements" is a *lagging* indicator to "training hours per internal auditor," it is a *leading* indicator for "percentage of audit recommendations implemented."

Another example of strategic objectives and performance measures for the innovation and capabilities perspective for internal audit functions is illustrated on the following page.

Innovation and Capabilities for Internal Audit Functions

Strategic Objective	Performance Measure
Provide thought leadership.	Number of best practices identified and communicated within the organization
Increase expertise and credentials of staff.	List and number of staff qualifications (certifications, education)
Encourage innovative practices within internal audit.	Number of innovative improvements implemented
Increase awareness and knowledge of best practices and business issues within the internal audit function.	Number of in-house trainings, presentations, and exercises
Increase awareness of business trends.	Monitoring of techniques to keep current with business unit trends

Adapt, Don't Adopt Philosophy

Examples such as the ones given in this chapter are very helpful for initiating thought processes. At the same time, it is essential to remember the importance of adapting, rather than adopting, a given approach. The frameworks and tools presented in this book should not be viewed simply as "plug-and-play" approaches. Any undertaking must be tailored to the organization. Therefore, practitioners should view the frameworks as tools, and their application should follow the philosophy of Dr. W. Edwards Deming, a founding father of total quality management (TQM), to adapt, not adopt.[3]

Too often, developing performance measures and scorecards can be an exercise in copying what others are doing. This often will miss the mark, as practices that work in one organization may not fit the needs or expectations of another. What is needed is to think strategically about how the internal audit function can create and protect value in its organization.

A very helpful tool for developing an internal audit department's strategic plan is The IIA's Practice Guide, Developing the Internal Audit Strategic Plan.[4] These examples focus on how the internal audit function can align its offerings with stakeholder and constituent needs.

Insight from Internal Audit Leaders

The following question-and-answer features provide insight about the keys to success for developing a Balanced Scorecard for an internal audit function. Insights are provided by:

- Joe Steakley, CAE at HCA Healthcare
- Greg Kalin, CAE at Morningstar
- Michael Pryal, vice president of internal audit at Federal Signal Corporation
- Jeff Perkins, vice president – Internal Audit at Transunion
- James Alexander, chief internal auditor and security officer at Unitus Community Credit Union

Aligning with Strategic Objectives and Risks

Joe Steakley, Chief Audit Executive, HCA Healthcare

Based on your experience, how would you describe the keys to success for developing scorecard performance measures that will reflect the strategic vision and value of internal auditing?

Closely align internal audit activities, organizational strategic objectives, industry changes, and emerging areas of risk. This process starts with the internal audit charter, including the department's purpose to the organization. The internal auditors should formally communicate the department's mission and vision at least annually, as well as ensure the scope of services is well defined and understood by key stakeholders. A Balanced Scorecard includes metrics related to fulfilling the mission and measuring progress toward the vision.

Another key to success is for the internal audit function to be closely involved with and, in many cases, to facilitate a comprehensive enterprisewide annual risk assessment. The risk-based audit plan should take into account the organization's risk management framework, including using risk appetite levels set by management and preparing the internal audit plan, based on the audit universe.

For internal audit to remain relevant by keeping up with existing and emerging challenges, the function should be front and center in the organization's identification and assessment of business risks and should think in terms of reinventing the purpose and vision of the internal audit function at least every five years.

What is an example of how the Balanced Scorecard and accompanying metrics can help to focus, monitor, and report on internal auditing's value?

A Balanced Scorecard and related metrics are the vehicles that allow internal audit to effectively communicate the value delivered to stakeholders on a periodic basis. For an internal audit function to be a leading and high-performing department, there should be proper alignment of the department's value proposition with key stakeholders' expectations. Over time, by consistently communicating the value of the internal audit function based on deliverables, the key stakeholders will perceive internal audit as operationally excellent, a key business partner, and a trusted advisor. Internal auditors should be seen as team members who are active in the business, members of any key steering committee for major organizational projects and initiatives, and perceived as highly collaborative, while maintaining independence and objectivity. An example of showcasing internal audit's value to the organization is conducting semiannual meetings with senior management, including the CEO and CFO, to report on the function's current activities and observations. This communication is best leveraged with a one-page "placemat" to communicate results, systemic issues, and other key findings. Our dashboard and executive summary communicate risk measurement to the organization by use of red, yellow, and green risk assessments. This example of monitoring and reporting puts a focus on ensuring the right people get the right message and highlighting the value of internal audit to stakeholders.

What advice (keys to success) would you give to CAEs to help them develop Balanced Scorecards and metrics?

- Make sure the department's Balanced Scorecard and metrics are simple, clear, and can be easily understood by stakeholders.

- Develop a risk-based audit plan mapped to the organization's strategy and mission.

- Maintain a consistent formal meeting process. Forums should focus on providing comprehensive reporting of audit results and organizational responses that showcase internal audit's value added to the organization.

- Annually communicate and map the internal audit activities to the organization's strategic agenda, showing the touch points and value added by internal audit.

- Always have a seat at the table and knowledge of the business, be visible, and maintain a balanced view.
- Continue to strategically evolve to align with industry changes and emerging risks, and focus on future areas of risk.

Meeting Stakeholders' Needs

Greg Kalin, Chief Audit Executive, Morningstar Inc.

Based on your experience, how would you describe the keys to success for developing scorecard performance measures that will reflect the strategic vision and value of internal auditing?

Successful internal audit departments must meet the needs of their stakeholders, including audit committees, executive management, operations personnel, and external auditors. These stakeholders, or customers, have very divergent opinions on what they expect from internal audit and what constitutes strategic vision and value. A successful Balanced Scorecard bridges the gap between these differing expectations and allows internal audit to measure its performance against a variety of metrics and expectations, and define its strategic value in a manner that can be understood and appreciated by all of its constituents.

What is an example of how the Balanced Scorecard and accompanying metrics can help to focus, monitor, and report on internal auditing's value?

We break our Quality Assurance and Improvement Program's Balanced Scorecard into three main categories: Governance, Professional Practice, and Communication. For example, Governance includes metrics for compliance with The IIA's International Professional Practices Framework and independence and objectivity, while Professional Practice contains metrics on the use of technology and staff certification. The Communication category measures audit engagement and client satisfaction, among others. Taken together, we measure 18 components within the three categories. Summarized together on a single page using red, yellow, and green buttons, the reader gets a clear snapshot of areas of success and areas in need of improvement.

The Balanced Scorecard

What advice (keys to success) would you give to CAEs to help them develop Balanced Scorecards and metrics?

To start, the CAE should understand what the stakeholders value in internal audit. Second, the CAE should select a mixture of quantitative and qualitative metrics that best define stakeholder values. To be successful, these metrics must be readily available. You may need to develop and perfect the metric collection and reporting mechanisms prior to designing the Balanced Scorecard. Finally, you need to design a manner for reporting the results of the Balanced Scorecard. The report should be brief, understandable, and informative.

Driving Positive Change

Michael Pryal, Vice President, Internal Audit, Federal Signal Corporation

Based on your experience, how would you describe the keys to success for developing scorecard performance measures that will reflect the strategic vision and value of internal auditing?

We have traditionally reported on common performance measures, such as report cycle times, satisfaction ratings, number of open vs. closed audit findings, etc. We are now expanding measures to highlight other support to the control environment, such as compliance and governance education, policy design assistance, and sharing of best practices. The internal audit function needs to determine and articulate how it is driving continual and positive change over risk and control behavior in the organization. This is key to our value proposition.

What is an example of how the Balanced Scorecard and accompanying metrics can help to focus, monitor, and report on internal auditing's value?

Over the past few years, we have enhanced our internal audit efforts to drive compliance education and facilitate understanding of global antifraud and anticorruption efforts. As such, we now regularly report to the audit committee our total training coverage and trends by business unit and employee group.

What advice (keys to success) would you give to CAEs to help them develop Balanced Scorecards and metrics?

Don't overkill it! Keep your measures simple and concise so your stakeholders can draw quick and meaningful conclusions on your function's value proposition (e.g., cost, quality of work, and how internal audit is driving positive change in the organization).

Using Qualitative Metrics

Jeff Perkins, Vice President — Internal Audit, TransUnion

Based on your experience, how would you describe the keys to success for developing scorecard performance measures that will reflect the strategic vision and value of internal auditing?

While developing internal audit performance measures at TransUnion, three key ingredients help ensure success:

1. Know the expectations of your stakeholders, as well as the basis for those expectations. At TransUnion, the primary stakeholders are the audit committee members and board of directors, along with the CEO and other senior executives. Various formal and informal methods are used to collaboratively discuss expectations.

2. Help educate the stakeholders regarding the objectives of the professional practice of internal auditing while also assessing their baseline understanding.

3. Match the expectations of the stakeholders with the current abilities, strategy, and vision of the internal audit department and ensure any alignment gaps are transparently discussed with the stakeholders, including ensuring that necessary revisions to the department's service/product delivery are timely addressed.

What is an example of how the Balanced Scorecard and accompanying metrics can help to focus, monitor, and report on internal auditing's value?

Key metrics have provided insightful information for both TransUnion's internal audit department and the primary stakeholders to help us adjust our audit schedule/plan on a real-time basis. While several metrics we monitor are quantitative in nature, qualitative metrics often provide deeper insight, especially as they relate to common industry or geographic risks. For instance, one of our measures involves monitoring how many significant risks occur to organizations other than TransUnion when those risks are not already included in the audit schedule. This metric includes an assessment of issues that develop at organizations outside of TransUnion and involves the root-cause analysis of industry risks to determine how well TransUnion is measuring up to our peers. For instance, in certain situations, risks encountered by other organizations become publically discussed and can serve as a strong basis for a deeper dive into certain controls and processes that may not be on the audit schedule. While our goal is to stay ahead of the curve when evaluating emerging risks, this type of benchmark can serve as a real-time adjustment to the audit plan and strategy, and should be discussed with the stakeholders.

What advice (keys to success) would you give to CAEs to help them develop Balanced Scorecards and metrics?

Focus on informal, subjective metrics, but also understand the importance of having consistent measures over time. Traditional quantitative measures should be a staple, but there may not be a readily available method to capture metrics for managing emerging risks to the success of internal audit. However, that should not prevent monitoring and reporting those trends and gut-level feelings to the stakeholders. Also, one of the best techniques in determining how we, as auditors, discuss and report metrics to our stakeholders is to communicate exactly as we would want to be communicated with by the process owners we audit, i.e., with transparency, honesty, timeliness, and a willingness to listen. (This also is how we self-assess our own processes with our stakeholders.)

Achieving Balance

James Alexander, Chief Internal Auditor & Security Officer,
Unitus Community Credit Union

What prompted you to develop a Balanced Scorecard at your company?

My company was using a Balanced Scorecard as part of its overall strategy. A key aspect to its approach was to balance not only earnings, but also service and people. As I began building the internal audit Balanced Scorecard, it clarified existing and needed performance measures that linked the strategy to the organization and key stakeholders.

How did you go about developing scorecard?

While I understood the theory and contributed to the organization's Balanced Scorecard, the resource that really helped me launch and build my department's scorecard was the 2002 IIARF research study, A Balanced Scorecard Framework for Internal Auditing Departments. This resource provided excellent information on how to develop an internal audit Balanced Scorecard with performance measures that link to the organization's strategy, and research on how peers were utilizing it and various types of performance measures.

What advice would you give to CAEs to help them develop a scorecard?

You have taken the first step which is to obtain this book. It provides excellent information for either creating or enhancing your existing internal audit Balanced Scorecard. Along with your organization's strategy and an internal audit strategy, it will make it very simple to create a Balanced Scorecard. You will want to review your Balanced Scorecard over time, so don't worry if it is not perfect on the first round.

Chapter 9

Using Strategy Maps for Risk Assessment and ERM

This chapter describes applications of the Balanced Scorecard and Strategy Maps in risk assessment and enterprise risk management (ERM). The strategic risk assessment process is presented to provide a way for internal auditors to focus on strategic risks. Strategy Maps are presented as a way to provide a comprehensive picture of the strategy and can serve as a reference point for identifying the various risks to it. The use of Strategy Maps in risk assessment also represents a valuable skill-set and capabilities that can be incorporated in the internal audit department's Balanced Scorecard. This chapter presents an example of a Strategy Map that integrates risk management strategic objectives. The strategic objectives relating to ERM may involve internal audit and provide opportunities for internal audit to create value in the process.

Strategic Risks are those risks that are most consequential to the organization's ability to execute its strategies and achieve its business objectives. Strategic Risk Assessment is a systematic and continual process for assessing significant risk facing an enterprise.

Derived from the Return Driven Strategy framework, the Strategic Risk Management framework provides a lens for addressing strategic risks and risk assessment, and developing a strategic risk profile.[1] The strategic risk assessment process discussed can be adapted by internal audit in applications of Strategy Maps for risk assessment, which are used to bridge the strategy of an enterprise and the risks. The chapter also discusses the development of a strategic risk management action plan and how the frameworks and tools presented in this book can be integrated in the strategic risk assessment process.

Strategic Risk Management Framework

As directors and management have used the Return Driven Strategy framework to evaluate the business strategy, they have been able to hone in on key risks that could destroy shareholder value while considering the upside of risk in terms of the opportunities, thereby using it as a *de facto* strategic risk management framework.[2]

The following characteristics make the Return Driven Strategy framework a good platform for risk assessment:

1. It is aligned with a commitment to ethically create shareholder wealth.

2. It is holistic and broad enough to encompass the spectrum of entitywide activities needed to achieve an organization's strategy.

3. It is capable of identifying and evaluating significant events and forces of change in terms of strategic business risk.

4. It has been vetted by management teams, boards, and thought leaders in risk management.

Figure 9.1 presents the strategic risk management framework, which represents the risk side of the Return Driven Strategy framework.

For each tenet in the Return Driven Strategy framework there is a corresponding risk. The strategic risks are driven from the failure to execute key tenets in the Return Driven Strategy framework:

- Failure to innovate offerings (tenet 5 in the Return Driven Strategy framework) drives innovation risk.

- Failure to partner deliberately and carefully (tenet 7 in the Return Driven Strategy framework) drives partnering risk.

- Failure to deliver offerings efficiently and effectively (tenet 4 in the Return Driven Strategy framework) drives operations risk.

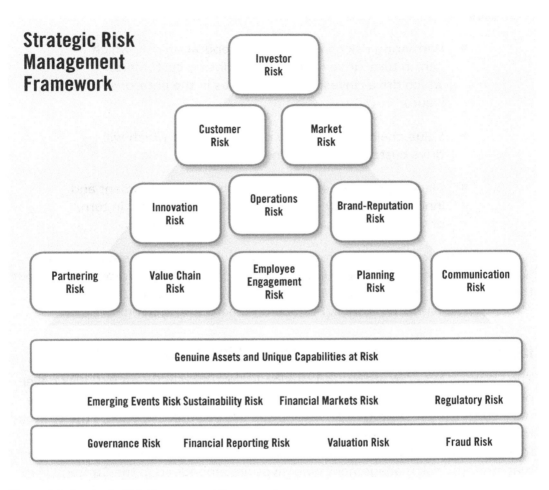

Figure 9.1. Strategic Risk Management Framework

©Copyright Mark L. Frigo and Richard J. Anderson 2009. Used with permission.

- Failure to ethically maximize wealth (tenet 1 of the Return Driven Strategy framework) by violating ethical parameters of constituents and communities can directly drive investor risk. (The market will severely punish unethical conduct.)

The strategic risks are also interrelated in a hierarchy. Here are some examples:

- Partnering risk can drive brand-reputation risk, which can, in turn, drive customer risk (losing customers), which drives investor risk (declines in the enterprise value).

- Value chain risk can drive operations risk, which will drive customer risk, which drives investor risk.

- Planning risk (in terms of research and development and innovation) can drive innovation risk, which can, in turn, drive customer risk, which can drive investor risk.

The Strategic Risk Management framework is used in the strategic risk assessment process presented in the next chapter. For more information about this framework, see *Strategic Risk Management: A Primer for Directors and Management Teams* by Mark L. Frigo and Richard J. Anderson.

Integrating Risk Management Strategic Objectives in Strategy Maps

The Strategy Map (an abstracted version is illustrated in **figure 9.2**) was developed by a management team as part of its strategic planning process, where the Return Driven Strategy framework was used to focus and align the strategy to the overall goal to create and protect shareholder value, and the Strategic Risk Management framework was used to develop a risk assessment.[3] Notice that strategic risk management objectives are embedded in the Strategy Map.

This Strategy Map includes some strategic objectives that are directly related to ERM, as shown in the internal process and capabilities and growth perspectives:

- Liabilities for failures: part of the operational excellence strategic theme

- Protect intellectual property: part of the create-value-with-technology theme

Using Strategy Maps for Risk Assessment and ERM

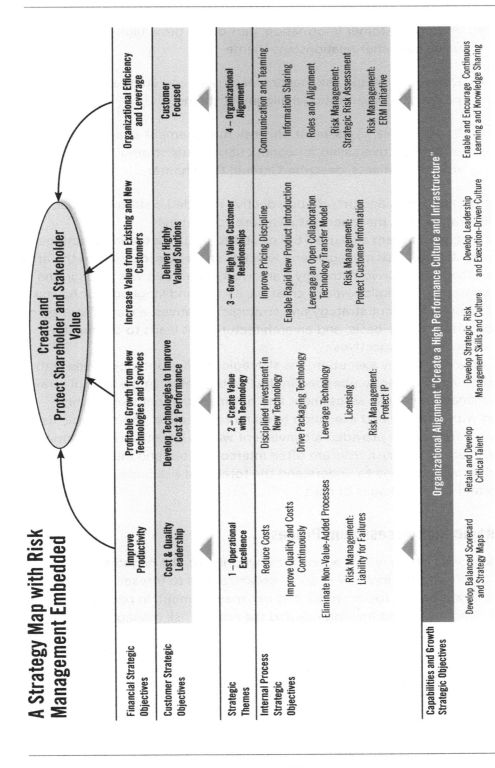

Figure 9.2. Strategy Map with Embedded Risk Management Objectives

Source: Frigo, Mark L. and Richard J. Anderson, Strategic Risk Management: A Primer for Directors and Management Teams (2010). Used with permission.

- Protect customer information: part of the grow high-value customer relationships theme

- Develop strategic risk management skills and culture: part of the organizational alignment theme

- Strategic risk assessment: this risk management strategic objective called for conducting annual strategic risk assessments, described later in this chapter

Also, the capabilities and growth perspective included a strategic objective to develop strategic risk management as a core competency.

The management team also used the exhibit to visualize the intersection of strategy and strategic risk management, which is strategy execution. In the area of strategy, the Return Driven Strategy framework provides a way to align the business strategy to optimize wealth creation; a logic and language for having an honest discussion about strategy and strategic initiatives; a way of strategic thinking on a day-to-day-basis; and an architecture that leads to organizing risks under the four perspectives.

In the area of strategy execution, the strategic themes and objectives with the four perspectives were embedded in the Strategy Map. In the area of strategic risk management, risk assessment and risk management were highly connected with strategy and execution to be more effective. The strategic risk management framework provided a convenient way to organize risk information and risk areas. Because risks are often interconnected and interrelated, the framework provided a way to understand the totality of risk impacts, as well as the cause-and-effect linkages of risks.

The Strategic Risk Assessment Process

One of the results of the recent economic environment, the negative economic events of 2008, and the inability of some organizations to foresee and manage risk is a new or renewed focus on risk and risk management. In particular, boards of directors are addressing risk and the related risk management practices of their organizations, and asking management tough questions about how the organization's risks are identified, assessed, monitored, and managed. Management teams are being challenged to respond and actively participate in risk assessments and risk management initiatives.

This new focus has spawned a variety of activities, including various types of risk assessments, ERM initiatives, or GRC initiatives. For many organizations, this heightened focus on risk is new and somewhat daunting to directors and management teams. Of particular concern is where to start and where the valuable time of directors and management should be directed to generate the maximum benefit to the organization.[4]

Focusing on Strategic Risk

Based on research and interactions with directors and senior executives, I suggest the right place for a board to start is the identification and management of *strategic risks*—those risks that are most consequential to the organizations' ability to execute its strategy and build and protect value. This strategic focus is not intended to identify every risk facing the organization, but it will identify those risks that are most significant to the organization's ability to achieve and realize its core business strategy and objectives. Accordingly, these risks should be of most concern to senior management and directors and most deserving of their time and attention. This focus on strategic risk also reinforces the direct relationship and critical linkage of the organization's strategy, strategy execution, and risk management processes.

A strategic risk assessment is designed to identify the organizations' strategic risks and related action plans to address those risks. Conducting an initial strategic risk assessment is a valuable activity, because understanding the organization's strategic risks is an important component of the responsibilities of the board. Current thought leadership on corporate governance and board responsibilities is virtually unanimous on a view that a key board responsibility is to understand the organization's strategies and the associated risks and ensure that management's risk management practices are appropriate.

For example, the National Association of Corporate Directors' recently published *Key Agreed Principles to Strengthen Corporate Governance for U.S. Publicly Traded Companies* states:

> For most companies, the priority focus of board attention and time will be understanding and providing guidance on *strategy and associated risk*...and monitoring senior management's performance in both carrying out the *strategy and managing risk.*

Chapter 10

How to Conduct a Strategic Risk Assessment

The strategic risk assessment process is designed as an approach that can be tailored to the specific needs and culture of the organization. To be most useful, a risk management process and resultant reporting must reflect and support the culture of the organization so that it can be embedded and owned by management. If the risk assessment and management processes are not embedded and owned by management as an integral part of their business processes, then the risk management process will rapidly lose its impact and not add or deliver on its expected role.[1]

Seven Steps for Conducting a Strategic Risk Assessment

As depicted in **figure 10.1**, the seven-step process for conducting a strategic risk assessment is:

1. Achieve a deep understanding of the strategy of the organization.
2. Gather views and data of strategic risks.
3. Prepare the preliminary strategic risk profile.
4. Validate and finalize the strategic risk profile.
5. Develop strategic risk management action plans.
6. Communicate the strategic risk profile and strategic risk management action plans.
7. Implement the strategic risk management action plans.[2]

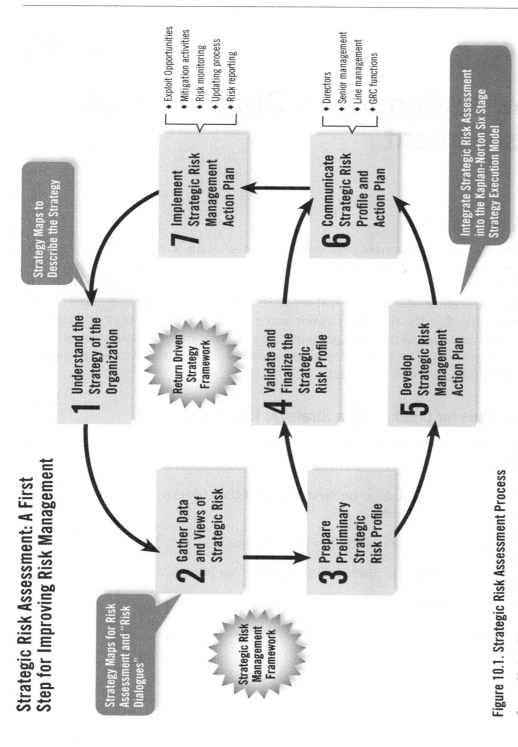

Figure 10.1. Strategic Risk Assessment Process

Source: Mark L. Frigo and Richard J. Anderson, "Strategic Risk Assessment: A First Step for Improving Risk Management and Governance," Strategic Finance (December 2009), www.imanet.org. Used with permission.

Strategy Maps can provide a view of the strategy and serve as a reference point for identifying the various risks to it, and can be incorporated in a strategic risk assessment. They can be used as the starting point for risk dialogues wherein management might ask, "What are the critical risks that could put attainment of this objective in jeopardy?" as suggested by Robert Kaplan and David Norton.[3] In step 1, the Strategy Map describes the strategy, and in step 2, it is used for gathering views on strategic risks.

While the steps define a basic, high-level process, they also allow for a significant amount of tailoring and customization in their execution to reflect the maturity and capabilities of the organization. The steps also reflect the fact that strategic risk assessment is an ongoing process, not just a one-time event. Reflecting the dynamic nature of risk, the seven steps constitute a circular or closed-loop process that should be ongoing and continual within the organization.

Accordingly, it is critical for the board and senior management to periodically conduct and agree on an assessment of the organization's strategic risks—those risks that are most consequential to the organization's ability to execute its strategies and achieve its business objectives. Typically, the strategic risk assessment is performed by management with input and validation by the directors. It is important in this assessment process to link the assessment of risk directly to the organization's strategies and strategy execution processes. The exact format of the assessment and the resulting strategic risk profile are dependent on the level of maturity of the organization's risk management processes. For example, organizations that are early in their development of risk management processes may find basic lists or matrices of risks useful, while organizations with more mature risk management processes may find more detailed or quantitative profiles more useful.

Step 1: Achieve a Deep Understanding of the Strategy of the Organization

The first step in the process is to develop a thorough understanding of the strategy of the organization and its key components. The focus here is to identify the specific risks associated with the core strategy, so it is important to have this deep understanding of the strategy and its key elements. To facilitate and give structure to this step, the Return Driven Strategy framework has been a useful tool (see Mark L Frigo and Joel Litman, DRIVEN: Business Strategy, Human Actions and the Creation of Wealth, 2007). This framework provides a way to analyze the strategy and identify, classify, and link its critical elements according to the framework's tenets and foundations. The process will, in later steps, allow a more detailed assessment of the risks associated with each tenet.

For example, one of the supporting tenets of the framework is to "partner deliberately." The assessment then needs to consider and identify any key initiatives in the organization's strategy where partnering is to be conducted. These initiatives may take many forms, including joint ventures, off-shoring, outsourcing, or other alliances. The organization may have many partnering arrangements, but the idea here is to identify the arrangements that are critical to the execution of the strategy and pinpoint their underlying strategic risks.

Much of the information for this step can be obtained from corporate and business unit plans, strategy summaries, and management and board materials. At the end of this step, the board and management should have a clearer understanding of the key elements of the organization's strategy as linked within the Return Driven Strategy framework.

This step can also include scenario planning, which can be used as way of embedding risk assessment in the business planning processes of a company. (For more information, see Mark L. Frigo and Hans Læssøe, "Strategic Risk Management at the LEGO Group," *Strategic Finance*, February 2012, 27–35. Anette Mikes and D. Hamel, "The LEGO Group: Envisioning Risks in Asia," Harvard Business School Case 9-113-054, November 2012. Anette Mikes and Migdal Amram, "The LEGO Group: Envisioning Risks in Asia (B)" Harvard Business School Case 9-114-048, 2013.)

Step 2: Gather Views and Data on Strategic Risks

In this step, the objective is to gather data and views from management and directors on the key strategic risks associated with the core business strategy. There are several ways to gather this information, including executive interviews, surveys, and focus groups. Here, the culture of the organization should be considered. Some organizations are very receptive to surveys, while others are not. If management is spread out geographically, individual interviews may be difficult, so teleconferencing or phone interviews may be used. Key members of management, including business-line leaders, should be asked to participate. It may also be useful to obtain the views of some members of the board, especially the audit committee. The organization's internal and external auditors also should be participants in this step.

Data gathering should also consider, review, and leverage information that is already available, such as risk assessments performed by internal groups like legal, compliance, or internal audit, or assessments performed related to compliance with the U.S. Sarbanes-Oxley Act of 2002. For public companies, their required risk disclosures should also be carefully reviewed.

Rather than simply asking an open question on what an individual considers to be a strategic risk, providing a structure or areas of focus can make the interviews more productive. Discussions and questions may be built from risk areas of the strategic risk management framework related to the strategy classifications defined in step 1.[4] The components of the strategic risk management framework correspond to the tenets of the Return Driven framework.

Another consideration is to use the philosophy of co-creation and the DART acronym in engaging stakeholders in risk assessment.[5] Co-creation rests on four key building blocks that create the DART acronym:

- D—Dialogue
- A—Access
- R—Risk-reward understanding
- T—Transparency (DART)

These four elements enable interactions among individuals and within processes to be more co-creative.[6] Through engagement platforms that are DART-enabled, organizations can:

- Engage all stakeholders in the co-creation of organizational purpose and decision making, thereby focusing on what stakeholders truly value and going beyond the conventional firm-centric view of product-service strategy.

- Reduce investment risk by leveraging the knowledge and skills of all stakeholders--both individually and as communities.

- Incorporate a more broad-based experience-centric view of value into their operations.

Participants should be encouraged to identify external risks that they believe would inhibit the organization's ability to achieve its strategic and business objectives. These external factors could include systemic risks, emerging risk areas, or other external factors, such as regulations. Participants also can be asked to rate the possible severity or impact of the risks they identify.

Step 3: Prepare a Preliminary Strategic Risk Profile

The information obtained in the first two steps is used to prepare a preliminary strategic risk profile of the organization. The exact format and complexity of the risk profile should be tailored to match the risk maturity and capabilities of the organization. Particularly for organizations just starting to formalize their risk management processes, keeping this profile straightforward and simple is important. This information is intended to spur discussion and understanding at executive and board levels, so excess detail or a large amount of data may be counterproductive. Many organizations find graphical presentations useful. For example, "heat maps" can use colors to convey levels of risk. Other organizations start with basic lists and then add detail and complexity as their risk processes mature.

Organizations also find it useful to communicate the potential level of exposure or impact associated with a risk area or type. Traditionally, probability and impact analyses were used. Recently, however, there has been concern about exposure to high-impact/low-probability risks ("black swan" events based on the book by Nassim Taleb), such as systemic risks that frequently have been overlooked because of their very low probability. For these types of risks, some organizations are adding new dimensions, such as the velocity of the risk or their organization's preparedness for the risk. Again, the level of detail and complexity of the strategic risk profile should mirror the maturity of the organization's risk management processes.

Step 4: Validate and Finalize the Strategic Risk Profile

Note: Although steps 4 and 5 are presented here in sequence, as reflected by the graphic, these steps are best executed in tandem.

The preliminary strategic risk profile must be validated with key participants to ensure that it is reflective of the participants' views of the key strategic risks. Again, the exact process that is used and in which participants are involved to validate the strategic risk profile may depend on the culture of the organization. Some organizations circulate the preliminary profile for comments, others conduct follow-up interviews, and still others use small group presentations and discussions. This validation process may include all stakeholder participants or only a portion of them. Possible risk profile reporting formats also can be circulated to get input and preferences. However, it is critically important to the entire assessment process that sufficient participants validate the profile and the risks highlighted.

Input and comments from this validation step can be used to make any needed revisions to the risk profile and report format. Validation is also an opportunity to build further buy-in to the entire strategic risk assessment process and the value to be obtained from the information gathered during the assessment.

Step 5: Develop Strategic Risk Management Action Plans

Once the strategic risks are identified, senior management and the directors will be quick to ask about plans to mitigate or monitor the risks. Accordingly, initial action plans should be developed and implemented as a core part of the assessment, rather than be developed later as a separate initiative. Again, the specific actions to be taken will depend on the maturity of the organization's risk management practices.

Based on work in the Strategic Risk Management Lab at DePaul University and various studies, it appears that many organizations are approaching risk management through a series of incremental steps, rather than moving directly to some desired end state. Organizations can use the *Strategic Risk Maturity Diagnostic* and the *Strategic Risk Alignment Guide* as tools to facilitate this step.[7]

Although specific actions to be taken depend on the exact situation of the organization, they typically will encompass some of the areas below:

- Mitigation activities to reduce some of the risks identified

- Risk monitoring activities to determine if risks are increasing or decreasing. (This may include such tools as Balanced Scorecards and Strategy Maps.)

- Plans for integrating strategic risk management tools in the strategy execution processes, such as the Kaplan-Norton Six-Stage Execution Process. (These six steps are listed at the end of this chapter.)

- A process to periodically update the strategic risk profile

- Various types of reporting activities

- Processes directed at the identification of new or emerging risks

This step is another opportunity to build cross-sharing of information and risk across the organization's various risk and control functions. The plans should address needed actions across the organization, not just within one risk or control function. This enterprisewide focus is another step toward building a strong risk management culture across the organization.

Step 6: Communicate the Strategic Risk Profile and Action Plans

At this stage of the assessment, the organization should have a validated strategic risk profile and initial action plans to address the strategic risks identified. Communication and building a common view of risk are widely accepted as leading practices in risk management. The Committee of Sponsoring Organizations of the Treadway Commission's (COSO's) *Enterprise Risk Management – Integrated Framework* includes "information and communication" as one of the eight core components of ERM.

This step challenges management to communicate throughout the enterprise the organization's view on its strategic risks and the importance of executing the related action plans. Communication must also flow upward to the directors as this is a topic requiring their attention and interaction. As stated by COSO (2004):

> The better the communications, the more effective a board will be in carrying out its oversight responsibilities—acting as a sounding board for management on critical issues, monitoring its activities, and providing advice, counsel, and direction. By the same token, the board should communicate its information needs to management and provide feedback and direction.

The organization should also consider its communication to external stakeholders, such as regulators, rating agencies, and shareholders. A recent progress report by Standard & Poor's on their initial reviews of ERM in nonfinancial companies indicated that:

> There appears to be a link between transparency and disclosure and companies' confidence about ERM; many companies have been willing and able to provide considerable detail about risk management practices.

Here again, the communication process represents an opportunity to build or reinforce the organization's risk culture. Various methods and means can be used to accomplish this communication, and it should be emphasized that successful communications are an iterative process.

Step 7: Implement the Strategic Risk Management Action Plans

The true value of the strategic risk assessment process lies in the resulting actions that the organization takes. These actions are intended to build the organization's ongoing strategic risk management processes and complete the circle. As noted above, the dynamic nature of risk requires ongoing processes to monitor and mitigate risk. Action plans should enable or enhance these processes.

The organization should consider how it reports and updates the status of the actions, including reporting to the board. As the organization continues to mature its strategic risk management processes, it should consider the next round of incremental steps to enhance its overall risk management processes. Following COSO's ERM framework, other major risk categories, such as operations and compliance, could be fruitful areas for subsequent risk initiatives.

Moving Forward with Strategic Risk Assessment

Internal auditors have a great opportunity to help boards of directors and senior management build the risk management processes of an organization focused on strategic risk, while aligning ERM and GRC initiatives based on an ongoing assessment of strategic risks. The strategic risk assessment can provide a necessary first step and foundation for risk management and governance, and help determine how risk will be assessed, monitored, and managed.

Strategic Risk Management Action Plan and Strategy Execution

The strategic risk management action plan should consider how risk assessment and risk management can be integrated in strategy-execution processes. This includes integrating risk management into strategic planning and performance measurement systems. The Kaplan-Norton Strategy Management System[8] described below provides a useful framework for visualizing where risk management can be integrated in strategy execution. Included is a brief discussion about how risk assessment and risk management can be embedded in the six stages.

Stage 1—Develop the Strategy

This stage includes developing mission, values, and vision; strategic analysis; and strategy formulation. At this stage, a strategic risk assessment can be included with the Return Driven Strategy framework to articulate the strategy, and the strategic risk management framework to identify strategic risks of the organization.

Stage 2—Translate the Strategy

This stage includes developing Strategy Maps, strategic themes, objectives, measures, targets, initiatives, Balanced Scorecards, and strategic expenditures. At this stage, the strategic risk management framework is useful in developing risk-based objectives and performance measures for the Balanced Scorecard and Strategy Map. It also is useful for analyzing risks related to strategic expenditures. The development of a risk scorecard can also be considered.

Stage 3—Align the Organization

This includes aligning business units, support units, employees, and boards of directors. At this stage, the strategic risk management alignment guide and strategic GRC framework are useful for aligning risk and control units toward more effective and efficient risk management and governance.

Stage 4—Plan Operations

This includes developing the operating plan, key process improvements, sales planning, resource capacity planning, and budgeting. In this stage, the strategic risk management action plan can be reflected in the operating plan and dashboards, including risk dashboards.

Stage 5—Monitor and Learn

This includes strategy reviews and operational reviews. In this stage, strategic risk reviews are part of the ongoing strategic risk assessment, which reinforces the necessary continual closed-loop approach for effective strategy risk assessment and strategy execution.

Stage 6—Test and Adapt

This stage includes profitability analysis and emerging strategies. In this stage, emerging risks can be considered as part of the ongoing strategic risk assessment.

For more information about the Kaplan-Norton Six-Stage Management System, see Robert S. Kaplan and David P. Norton, *The Execution Premium: Linking Strategy to Operations for Competitive Advantage* (Boston, MA: Harvard Business School Press, 2008).

For more information about strategy risk management action plans, see Mark L. Frigo and Richard J. Anderson, *Strategic Risk Management: A Primer for Directors and Management Teams* (2010).

Strategic Risk Management Tools

Strategic risk management is a process for identifying, assessing, and managing risk anywhere in the strategy with the ultimate goal of protecting and creating shareholder value. It is a primary component and foundation of ERM effected by boards of directors, management, and other personnel. It requires a strategic view of risk and consideration of how external and internal events or scenarios will affect the ability of the organization to achieve its objectives; requires an organization to define a tolerable level of risk or risk appetite as a guide for strategic decision making; and is a continual process that should be embedded in strategy setting and strategy management.

1. Return Driven Strategy Framework

This framework is used in Step 1 to analyze the elements of the organizations' strategy. It provides a systematic way and a common language for articulating and clarifying the strategy of the organization. It also provides a lens for understanding how various elements of the strategy link together and drive value creation, while bringing perspective to identifying risk areas in the strategy.[9]

2. Strategic Risk Management Framework

This framework for accessing strategic risk has been vetted by directors, management teams, and thought leaders in ERM and GRC. It provides a way to identify, link, and prioritize a broad spectrum of strategic risks to the organization, including innovation risk, operations risk, brand and reputation risk, partnering risk, supply chain risk, employee engagement risk, and unique capabilities (genuine assets) as risk.[10]

3. Strategic GRC Framework

This framework provides an overview for aligning risk and control units in an organization.[11]

(For more information on strategic risk assessments, see Frigo and Anderson, *Strategic Risk Management: A Primer for Directors and Management Teams*, 2010.)

Chapter 11

Summary and Conclusions

This book presented management tools and strategy frameworks to assist internal auditors in reflecting, communicating, and executing a valuable strategic vision through the application of the Balanced Scorecard framework and Strategy Maps. Those applications include:

- Developing a strategy for the internal audit function using the Return Driven Strategy. framework and Mission Driven Strategy framework

- Developing a Balanced Scorecard for the internal audit function

- Applications of the Strategy Maps in risk assessment and ERM

A Final Word

One of the fundamental questions that audit committee chairs ask is, "How do I know my internal audit function is effective?" CAEs should address this question when reviewing and developing their function's strategy and performance measures and establishing a Balanced Scorecard. The question-and-answer features at the end of this chapter explore this issue and serve as a conclusion to this book.

After all, when used to meet its best potential, the Balanced Scorecard, in essence, ultimately can provide evidence of internal audit effectiveness and reflect the strategic vision and value of an internal audit function.

Insight from Internal Audit Leaders

The following question-and-answer features offer further perspective about developing a strategy and Balanced Scorecard focused on internal audit effectiveness. David Landsittel, former COSO chairman, discusses how internal audit strategy can be linked to enterprise strategy. Kathy Robinson, CAE at ADP, provides insight about internal audit effectiveness, strategy, and scorecards. As a finale, Dick Anderson, clinical professor of strategic risk management at DePaul University, discusses the three most important dimensions of internal audit effectiveness.

Summary and Conclusions

Linking Internal Audit Strategy to Enterprise Strategy

David L. Landsittel, Former COSO chairman, Former Molex Incorporated Audit Committee Chair, Former AICPA Auditing Standards Board Chair

Based on your experience as a director, how would you describe the most important dimensions of internal audit effectiveness?

I think the overriding indicator of internal audit effectiveness is the extent to which the function commands respect throughout the organization, so that business units and functional leaders do not look at the function as being pushed on them, but one that is demanded by them to assist in building value.

What advice would you give to CAEs in developing a strategy for internal audit that is linked with the strategy of the enterprise?

Importantly, as an audit committee chair, my first concern is that the function focuses on the compliance function—and in a way that takes advantage of innovative trends (e.g., continuous monitoring, data analytics) to drive compliance efficiency and effectiveness. That needs to be balanced with a strategic consulting role, with the function's limited resources focusing on highest valued options—i.e., those strategic risks that might cause the highest market value decrease.

What advice would you give to CAEs in developing internal audit Balanced Scorecard performance measures relating to internal audit function effectiveness?

As an audit committee chair, I would suggest that the performance measures focus on:

- Vision and strategy that are aligned with stakeholder expectations
- Appropriate level of audit resources

- Innovation that drives efficiency and effectiveness
- Talent development
- A risk-based audit plan that is linked to both stakeholder expectations and ERM results
- Effective project management
- Effective relationships with key stakeholders
- Branding to develop a value-based "demand pull" function
- Quality assurance and continuous improvement in the effectiveness of internal audit functions

Summary and Conclusions

Developing Balanced Scorecards to Reflect the Strategic Vision of Internal Audit

Kathy Robinson, Chief Audit Executive, ADP

Based on your experience as a director how would you describe the most important dimensions of internal audit effectiveness?

Just like a business function, the key is to understand what the strategic objectives are and what can impede the achievement of those objectives. Internal audit functions come in all shapes and sizes. What is unique about your value drivers and how is that linked to the department strategy and the strategic vision for the company? Start there.

What advice would you give to CAEs in developing a strategy for internal audit that is linked with the strategy of the enterprise?

I think the key word here is "focus." There are so many initiatives to monitor, tasks to execute, and meetings to attend. A Balanced Scorecard aligned to the department's vision keeps everyone in lock step. It alerts audit management when there is slippage or where there may be excess capacity. It also provides a visual reminder that audit is a team sport; we can achieve more by working together, than individually.

What advice would you give to CAEs in developing internal audit Balanced Scorecard performance measures?

Determine your value drivers for the organization and then test that hypothesis with your key stakeholders. I have found conversations with executive leadership and the board that result in actions to position the internal auditors as those who can influence and drive innovative change are always well received.

Three Important Dimensions of Internal Audit Effectiveness

Richard J. (Dick) Anderson, Partner (Retired), PricewaterhouseCoopers LLP, Clinical Professor of Strategic Risk Management, DePaul University

What are the most important dimensions of internal audit effectiveness?

1. Effectively meeting the expectations of the key stakeholders of internal audit is the first and most important dimension of internal audit effectiveness.

    To accomplish this, CAEs must first have a clear and agreed-upon understanding of the expectations of their key stakeholders—specifically the audit committee and executive management. The expectations should be articulated, validated by the key stakeholders, and then used to drive the direction and activities of the internal audit function.

2. Operating in a highly effective manner using leading or best practices in the delivery of its services is the second dimension of effectiveness.

    This involves identifying leading practices and activities that would facilitate internal audit's ability to meet and exceed the expectations of its key stakeholders. In identifying specific possible actions or practices, the stakeholder expectations serve as the filter. There should be direct linkage between the practices being used or developed and the achievement of stakeholder expectations. In addition, constant improvement and innovation should be part of this dimension.

3. Meeting applicable professional and regulatory standards and requirements is the third dimension of effectiveness.

    Internal audit also needs to ensure that it meets internal audit professional standards and any applicable regulatory or legal requirements. For most internal audit functions, this means conforming to the requirements of the *International Standards for the Professional Practice of Internal Auditing* (*Standards*) as promulgated by The IIA. Certain industries, such as banking, have additional regulatory requirements that internal audit must effectively meet. However, CAEs also should remember that standards are more foundational than aspirational, and will not, by themselves, ensure that an internal audit function is highly effective.

What advice would you give to CAEs in developing internal audit Balanced Scorecard performance measures relating to these three aspects of internal audit effectiveness?

Internal audit performance measure must address each of the three dimensions noted above. While most internal audit functions have some measures designed to ensure effectiveness of operations and compliance with standards, the key is really developing specific performance measures that address the unique expectations of their key stakeholders. Those measures are usually the hardest to develop, but in the end, they are much more significant than the others.

Appendix A

The IIA's Imperatives for Change

The IIA report, *Imperatives for Change: The IIA's Global Internal Audit Survey in Action: A Component of the CBOK Study (2011),* can be viewed through the lens of the Return Driven Strategy and Mission Driven Strategy frameworks as a platform for developing the strategy of an internal audit department.[1] The imperatives comprise four groups, as detailed below.

Group I: Emphasize Risk Management and Governance

1. Sharpen Focus on Risk Management & Governance
2. Conduct a More Responsive & Flexible Risk-Based Audit Plan

Group II: Address Key Stakeholder Priorities

3. Develop a Strategic Vision for Internal Auditing
4. Focus, Monitor, & Report on Internal Auditing's Value
5. Strengthen Audit Committee Communications & Relationships
6. View Standards Compliance as Mandatory, Not Optional

Group III: Optimize Internal Audit Resources

    7. Acquire & Develop Top Talent

    8. Enhance Training for Internal Audit Functions

    9. Take Advantage of Expanding Service Provider Membership

Group IV: Leverage Technology Effectively

    10. 10. Step up Your Use of Audit Technology and Tools

Each of these imperatives has implications for the development of the strategy and scorecard performance measures for internal audit. For example, the Group I imperative to sharpen focus on risk management and governance can be used to guide the development of strategic objectives and performance measures in a Balanced Scorecard, as CAEs execute risk management and governance initiatives. The Group II imperatives support the need of a clear strategy. The Group III imperatives are relevant for developing strategic objectives and performance measure in the innovation and capabilities perspective of the Balanced Scorecard. And Group IV's imperative can guide the development of strategic objectives and performance measures relating to audit technology initiatives.

Appendix B
History of the Balanced Scorecard

The original 12 companies studied in the 1990 Kaplan and Norton study included Advanced Micro Devices, American Standard, Apple Computer, Bell South, CIGNA, Conner Peripherals, Cray Research, DuPont, Electronic Data Systems, General Electric, Hewlett-Packard, and Shell Canada. A summary of that study was published in an article in the *Harvard Business Review* in 1992, which led to a second wave of development of the Balanced Scorecard model.[1] *The Balanced Scorecard: Translating Strategy into Action* by Kaplan and Norton summarized the developments and case scenarios of Balanced Scorecard initiatives.[2]

As the Balanced Scorecard has continued to develop and evolve, the adoption of the framework has rapidly and pervasively spread across industry groups, including retailers, manufacturers, financial services, technology, and other industries. In 1998, a study conducted by the Institute of Management Accountants found that more than 40 percent of the companies use a Balanced Scorecard approach.[3] A study by Bain & Company in 1999 found that approximately 50 percent of the Fortune 1000 companies in North America and 45 percent of companies in Europe were using the Balanced Scorecard.[4] And in 1997, the *Harvard Business Review* designated the Balanced Scorecard as one of the most important management practices in the last 75 years. Kaplan and Norton's 2001 book, *The Strategy-Focused Organization*, reflected the continuing evolution of this innovative model and presented five principles of the strategy-focused organization.[5] The introduction of *Strategy Maps* took the concepts deeper.[6]

A 2006 book by Kaplan and Norton elaborated on alignment, which represents principle 3 (aligning all organizational units to the strategy) for the strategy-focused organization.[7] In this book, they focus on the importance of alignment in getting the most out of using Balanced Scorecards.[8] This pertains to not only alignment of units within an organization, but also alignment among the firm and its board, investors, customers, and suppliers.

This concept includes aligning:

- Financial and customer strategies[9]
- Internal processes and learning and growth strategies[10]
- Support functions[11]

The Balanced Scorecard represents a way organizations can describe, communicate, measure, and manage strategy. It impacts strategic areas such as human resources,[12] and has been applied to measuring the performance of corporate boards.[13] It also can be used to evaluate and refine strategy at the departmental level. For example, a 2002 IIARF study examined how the Balanced Scorecard could be used to refine the strategy of an internal audit department and align it with audit committee and corporate priorities.[14]

The History and Continuing Evolution of the Balanced Scorecard Framework

1990—One-Year Study, "Measuring the Organization of the Future" (Kaplan and Norton)

1992—First *Harvard Business Review* article, "The Balanced Scorecard: Measures That Drive Performance"

1993—Second *Harvard Business Review* article, "Putting the Balanced Scorecard to Work"

1996—First Balanced Scorecard book by Kaplan and Norton, *The Balanced Scorecard,* published by Harvard Business School Press

1997—The Balanced Scorecard is noted as one of the most important management practices in "75 Years of Management Ideas and Practices 1922–1997" in *Harvard Business Review*

1998—Institute of Management Accountants study (Frigo and Krumwiede) finds 40% of companies are using the Balanced Scorecard

1999—Bain & Company study finds 55% of large companies are using the Balanced Scorecard

2000—Second Balanced Scorecard book by Kaplan and Norton, *The Strategy-Focused Organization,* published by Harvard Business School Press

2004—Third Balanced Scorecard book by Kaplan and Norton, *Strategy Maps,* published by Harvard Business School Press

2006—Fourth Balanced Scorecard book by Kaplan and Norton, *Alignment*, published by Harvard Business School Press

2008—Fifth Balanced Scorecard book by Kaplan and Norton, *The Execution Premium: Linking Strategy to Operations for Competitive Advantage*, including accumulated lessons from the previous 15 years and a description of how the framework has become the number one management system for strategy execution

2012—The 20th anniversary of the introduction of the Balanced Scorecard and its continuing evolution[15]

Notes

Chapter 1: Introduction

1. Mark L. Frigo, "The Balanced Scorecard: Twenty Years and Counting," *Strategic Finance,* October 2012, 49–53.

Chapter 2: The Balanced Scorecard Framework

1. Mark L. Frigo, "The Balanced Scorecard: 20 Years and Counting," *Strategic Finance,* October 2012, 49–53.

2. Robert S. Kaplan and David P. Norton, "The Balanced Scorecard: Measures that Drive Performance," *Harvard Business Review* 70, no 1 (January–February 1992): 71–79. Robert S. Kaplan and David P. Norton, *The Balanced Scorecard: Translating Strategy into Action* (Boston: Harvard Business Review Press, 1996).

3. Robert S. Kaplan and David P. Norton, *The Execution Premium: Linking Strategy to Operations for Competitive Advantage* (Boston, MA: Harvard Business Review Press, 2008).

4. See Robert S. Kaplan and David P. Norton, "The Balanced Scorecard: Measures that Drive Performance." Robert S. Kaplan and David P. Norton, "Putting the Balanced Scorecard to Work," *Harvard Business Review* 71, no. 5 (September–October 1993): 134–142. Robert S. Kaplan and David P. Norton, "Using the Balanced Scorecard as a Strategic Management System," *Harvard Business Review* 74, no. 1 (January–February 1996): 75–85. Robert S. Kaplan and David P. Norton, *The Balanced Scorecard: Translating Strategy into Action* (Boston, MA: Harvard Business School Press, 1996).

5. Robert S. Kaplan and David P. Norton, "Having Trouble with Your Strategy? Then Map It," *Harvard Business Review* 78, no. 5 (September–October 2000): 167–176. Robert S. Kaplan and David P. Norton, *Strategy Maps: Converting Intangible Assets into Tangible Outcomes* (Boston, MA: Harvard Business School Press, 2004).

The Balanced Scorecard

6. See Robert S. Kaplan and David P. Norton, "The Balanced Scorecard: Measures That Drive Performance." Robert S. Kaplan and David P. Norton, "Putting the Balanced Scorecard to Work," 134–147. Robert S. Kaplan and David P. Norton, "Using the Balanced Scorecard as a Strategic Management System," *Harvard Business Review* 74, no. 1 (January–February 1996): 75–85. Robert S. Kaplan and David P. Norton, *The Balanced Scorecard: Translating Strategy into Action.* Robert S. Kaplan and David P. Norton, *The Strategy-Focused Organization: How Balanced Scorecard Companies Thrive in the New Business Environment* (Boston, MA: Harvard Business School Publishing, 2001). Robert S. Kaplan and David P. Norton. "Having Trouble with Your Strategy? Then Map It." Robert S. Kaplan and David P. Norton, *Strategy Maps: Converting Intangible Assets into Tangible Outcomes.*

7. Robert S. Kaplan and David P. Norton, *Strategy Maps: Converting Intangible Assets into Tangible Outcomes.*

8. Robert S. Kaplan and David P. Norton, "The Balanced Scorecard and Nonprofit Organizations" *Balanced Scorecard Report,* November–December 2002. Chapter 5 in Robert S. Kaplan and David P. Norton, *The Strategy-Focused Organization: How Balanced Scorecard Companies Thrive in the New Business Environment.* P. R. Niven, *Balanced Scorecard Step by Step for Government and Nonprofit Agencies* (New York: John Wiley & Sons, 2002).

9. Robert S. Kaplan and David P. Norton, *Strategy Maps: Converting Intangible Assets into Tangible Outcomes*, xii–xiii.

10. Mark L. Frigo, "Performance Measures that Drive the First Tenet of Business Strategy," *Strategic Finance*, September 2003, 8–11.

11. Mark L. Frigo, "Performance Measures that Drive the Goal Tenets of Strategy," *Strategic Finance,* October 2003, 9–11.

12. Robert S. Kaplan and David P. Norton, *Strategy Maps: Converting Intangible Assets into Tangible Outcomes*, 379–381.

13. Michael E. Porter, *Competitive Advantage: Creating and Sustaining Superior Performance* (New York: The Free Press, 1985).

14. Robert S. Kaplan and David P. Norton, *Strategy Maps: Converting Intangible Assets into Tangible Outcomes*, 203.

Chapter 3: Strategy Maps

1. Robert S. Kaplan and David P. Norton, *Strategy Maps: Converting Intangible Assets into Tangible Outcomes* (Boston, MA: Harvard Business School Press, 2004). Mark L. Frigo, "The Value of Strategy Maps," *Strategic Finance,* March 2004, 23–25.

Notes

Chapter 4: Guidelines for Using Balanced Scorecards to Manage and Measure Performance

1. Mark L. Frigo, "Strategy-Focused Performance Measures," *Strategic Finance,* September 2002, 10-15.

2. Michael Porter, "The Importance of Being Strategic," *Balanced Scorecard Report* (March–April 2002).

3. Robert S. Kaplan and David P. Norton, *The Execution Premium* (Boston, MA: Harvard Business School Press, 2008).

Chapter 5: Return Driven Strategy Framework

1. This chapter is adapted from the book by Mark L. Frigo and Joel Litman, *DRIVEN: Business Strategy, Human Actions, and the Creation of Wealth* (Chicago: Strategy & Execution, 2007). The Return Driven Strategy framework is copyrighted by Mark L. Frigo and Joel Litman. Return Driven Strategy is the registered service mark of Mark L. Frigo, PhD, in the United States Patent and Trademark Office.

2. Mark L. Frigo and Richard J. Anderson, "10 Steps to Implement the Strategic GRC Framework," *Internal Auditor,* June 2009, 33-37. Used by permission.

3. Mark L. Frigo and Joel Litman, *DRIVEN: Business Strategy, Human Actions, and the Creation of Wealth.*

4. Ibid.

Chapter 6: Mission Driven Strategy Framework

1. Mark L. Frigo, *Mission Driven Strategy: A Primer for Management Teams,* 2011. Mark. L. Frigo "Mission Driven Strategy," *Strategic Finance,* August 2003, 8-11.

2. Gary Hamel and C. K. Prahalad, "Strategic Intent," *Harvard Business Review 67,* no. 3 (May–June 1989): 63-78.

3. Jim Collins, *Good to Great: Why Some Companies Make the Leap…And Others Don't* (New York: Harper Business, 2001).

4. Jim Collins, "Best New Year's Resolution? A 'Stop Doing' List," *USA Today,* December 30, 2003.

Chapter 7: A Strategic GRC Framework

1. This chapter is adapted from Mark L. Frigo and Richard J. Anderson, "Strategic GRC: 10 Steps to Implementation," *Internal Auditor,* June 2009, 33-37.

Chapter 8: Developing a Balanced Scorecard for the Internal Audit Function

1. Porter, Michael. "What Is Strategy?" *Harvard Business Review,* November–December, 1996.

2. The discussion of the Balanced Scorecard for internal audit is based on Mark L. Frigo, *A Balanced Scorecard Framework for Internal Auditing Departments* (Altamonte Springs, FL: The Institute of Internal Auditors Research Foundation, 2000), 46–53.

3. W. Edwards Deming, *Out of the Crisis* (Boston, MA: The MIT Press, 2000).

4. IIA Practice Guide, Developing the Internal Audit Strategic Plan (Altamonte Springs, FL: The Institute of Internal Auditors, 2012).

Chapter 9: Using Strategy Maps for Risk Assessment and ERM

1. Portions of this chapter are based on material drawn from the following sources: Mark L. Frigo and Richard J. Anderson, "Strategic Risk Assessment: A First Step for Improving Risk Management and Governance," *Strategic Finance,* December 2009, 25–33. Mark L. Frigo and Richard J. Anderson, "Strategic Risk Management: A Primer for Directors," Director Notes (The Conference Board), July 2012. Mark L. Frigo and Richard J. Anderson, *Strategic Risk Management: A Primer for Directors and Management Teams,* 2010.

2. Mark L. Frigo and Mark Beasley, "Strategic Risk Management: Creating and Preserving Value," *Strategic Finance,* May 2007.

3. Mark L. Frigo and Richard J. Anderson, *Strategic Risk Management: A Primer for Directors and Management Teams.*

4. This section is adapted from Mark L. Frigo and Richard J. Anderson, "Strategic Risk Assessment: A First Step for Improving Risk Management and Governance."

Chapter 10: How to Conduct a Strategic Risk Assessment

1. This chapter was adapted from Mark L. Frigo and Richard J. Anderson, "Strategic Risk Assessment: A First Step for Improving Risk Management and Governance," *Strategic Finance,* December 2009, with the permission of *Strategic Finance* and the Institute of Management Accountants, www.imanet.org.

2. Mark L. Frigo and Richard J. Anderson, "Strategic Risk Assessment: A First Step for Improving Risk Management and Governance," 25–33.

3. Mark L. Frigo, "The Balanced Scorecard: Twenty Years and Counting," *Strategic Finance,* October 2012, 49–53.

4. Mark L. Frigo, "When Strategy and ERM Meet," *Strategic Finance,* January 2008. Mark S. Beasley and Mark L. Frigo, "Strategic Risk Management: Creating and Protecting Value," *Strategic Finance,* May 2007.

5. Mark L. Frigo and Venkat Ramaswamy, "Co-Creating Strategic Risk-Return Management," *Strategic Finance,* May 2009.

6. For more information about co-creation see C. K. Prahalad and Venkat Ramaswamy, *The Future of Competition: Co-Creating Unique Value with Customers* (Boston, MA: Harvard Business School Press, 2004). Venkat Ramaswamy and Francis Gouillart, *The Power of Co-Creation: Build It with Them to Boost Growth, Productivity, and Profits* (New York: Free Press, 2010). Venkat Ramaswamy and K. Ozcan, "The Co-Creation Paradigm" (Palo Alto, CA: Stanford University Press, 2014, forthcoming).

7. For more information about the Strategic Risk Maturity Diagnostic and the Strategic Risk Alignment Guide, see Mark L. Frigo and Richard J. Anderson, *Strategic Risk Management: A Primer for Directors and Management Teams,* 2010.

8. Robert S. Kaplan and David P. Norton, *The Execution Premium: Linking Strategy to Operations for Competitive Advantage* (Boston, MA: Harvard Business School Press, 2008).

9. Mark L. Frigo, "Return Driven: Lessons for High Performance Companies," *Strategic Finance,* July 2008. Mark L. Frigo and Joel Litman, *DRIVEN: Business Strategy, Human Actions, and the Creation of Wealth* (Strategy & Execution, 2007).

10. Mark L. Frigo and Richard J. Anderson, *Strategic Risk Management: A Primer for Directors and Management Teams.*

11. Mark L. Frigo and Richard J. Anderson, "A Strategic Framework for GRC," *Strategic Finance*, February 2009.

Appendix A: The IIA's Imperatives for Change

1. *Imperatives for Change: The IIA's Global Internal Audit Survey in Action: A Component of the CBOK Study* (Altamonte Springs, FL: The Institute of Internal Auditors Research Foundation, 2011).

Appendix B: History of the Balanced Scorecard

1. Robert S. Kaplan and David P. Norton, "The Balanced Scorecard–Measures that Drive Performance," *Harvard Business Review,* January–February 1992, 71–79.

2. Robert S. Kaplan and David P. Norton, *The Balanced Scorecard: Translating Strategy into Action* (Boston, MA: Harvard Business School Press, 1996).

3. Mark L. Frigo, "The State of Strategic Performance Measurement: The IMA 2001 Survey," *The Balanced Scorecard Report* (Boston, MA: Harvard Business School Press, November–December 2001), 13–14.

4. Darrell Rigby, *Management Tools and Techniques* (Bain & Company, 1999).

5. Robert S. Kaplan and David P. Norton, *The Strategy-Focused Organization: How Balanced Scorecard Companies Thrive in the New Business Environment* (Boston, MA: Harvard Business School Publishing, 2001).

6. Robert S. Kaplan and David P. Norton, *Strategy Maps: Converting Intangible Assets into Tangible Outcomes* (Boston, MA: Harvard Business School Press, 2004).

7. Robert S. Kaplan and David P. Norton, *Alignment: Using the Balanced Scorecard to Create Corporate Synergies* (Boston, MA: Harvard Business School Press, 2006).

8. Ibid.

9. Ibid, chapter 3.

10. Ibid, chapter 4.

11. Ibid, chapter 5.

12. Brian E. Becker, Mark A. Huselid, and Dave Ulrich, *The HR Scorecard: Linking People, Strategy, and Performance* (Boston, MA: Harvard Business School Press, 2001).

13. M. J. Epstein and M. J. Roy, "How Does Your Board Rate?" *Strategic Finance,* February 2004, 25–31. M. J. Epstein and M. J. Roy, *Measuring and Improving the Performance of Corporate Boards* (The Society of Management Accountants of Canada, 2001).

14. Mark L. Frigo, *A Balanced Scorecard for Internal Auditing Departments* (Altamonte Springs, FL: The Institute of Internal Auditors Research Foundation, 2002).

15. Mark L. Frigo, "The Balanced Scorecard: 20 Years and Counting," *Strategic Finance,* 2012, 49–53.

Glossary

Balanced Scorecards. Include strategic objectives and performance measures in a hierarchy that includes financial, customer, internal process, and learning and growth perspectives.

Baseline Performance. The current level of performance for the performance measure. An example of a baseline performance for "Percentage of Total Revenue from New Product Offerings" would be 15 percent.

Cause-and-Effect Linkages. Performance measures are connected using cause-and-effect linkages. Performance measures include Performance Drivers (leading indicators) and Outcome Performance Measures (lagging indicators).

Four Perspectives of the Balanced Scorecard. The four perspectives of the Balanced Scorecard include:

> **Customer Perspective.** This perspective focuses on customer performance in areas that are most critical to the customer. Examples of performance measures include customer satisfaction and customer retention.
>
> **Financial Perspective.** This perspective focuses on return on investment and other supporting financial performance measures. Examples of performance measures include profitability, return on invested capital, and revenue growth.
>
> **Internal Business Processes Perspective.** This perspective focuses on operating effectively and efficiently and includes performance measures on cost, quality, and time for processes that are critical to the customers. Examples of performance measures include number of defects and cycle time.

Learning and Growth Perspective. This perspective focuses on performance measures relating to employees, infrastructure, teaming, and capabilities necessary for the internal processes to achieve customer performance and financial results. Examples of performance measures include employee satisfaction, employee engagement, hours of training per employee, and information technology expenditures per employee.

Performance Measures. Describe how success in achieving the strategy will be measured and tracked for a particular strategic objective. An example of a performance measure would be "percentage of total revenue from new product offerings."

Strategic Initiatives (Action Plans). Key action programs or action plans required to achieve strategic objectives. They describe the details of what actions need to be taken, timelines for the actions, responsibility of taking the action steps, and resources for getting the action plan done.

Strategic Objectives. These are word statements of what the strategy must achieve and what is critical to success. Strategic objectives describe the strategy of the organization and are included in the four perspectives of the Balanced Scorecard. An example of a strategic objective in the financial perspective for a growth strategic initiative would be "increase revenue from new product offerings."

Strategic Risks. Those risks that are most consequential to the organization's ability to execute its strategies and achieve its business objectives.

Strategic Themes. Strategic themes generally involve growth and productivity themes. Both should be represented in a Balanced Scorecard framework. For example, a strategic theme could be "grow revenue from international sales" for a growth strategic theme, or "improve asset utilization" for a productivity strategic theme. A Balanced Scorecard should have both growth and productivity strategic themes represented and described.

Strategy Maps. Describe the strategy of the organization and the cause-and-effect linkages between the strategic objectives.

Targets. The level of performance or rate of improvement needed in the performance measure often using "stretch targets," which provide a target that is challenging yet attainable. An example of a target performance for "percentage of total revenue from new product offerings" would be 20 percent (versus 15 percent baseline performance).

Bibliography

Anderson, Richard J., and Mark L. Frigo. "What Should Directors Ask about Risk Management?" *Strategic Finance,* April 2012, 17–20.

Beasley, Mark S., and Mark L. Frigo. "Strategic Risk Management: Creating and Preserving Value." *Strategic Finance,* May 2007, 25–53.

Beasley, Mark S., and Mark L. Frigo. "Strategic Risk Management: Creating and Protecting Value." *Singapore Accountant,* January–February 2008.

Beasley, Mark, et al. "Working Hand in Hand: Balanced Scorecards and Enterprise Risk Management." *Strategic Finance,* March 2006, 49–55.

Becker, Brian E., Mark A. Huselid, and Dave Ulrich. *The HR Scorecard: Linking People, Strategy, and Performance.* Boston, MA: Harvard Business School Press, 2001.

PricewaterhouseCoopers. *Building a Strategic Internal Audit Function.* PricewaterhouseCoopers, 2009.

Busco, Cristiano, Mark L. Frigo, and Robert W. Scapens. "Beyond Compliance: Why Integrated Governance Matters Today." *Strategic Finance,* August 2005, 34–43.

Charan, Ram. *Owning Up: The 14 Questions Every Board Member Needs to Ask.* Hoboken, NJ: John Wiley & Sons, 2009.

Cokins, Gary. *Performance Management: Finding the Missing Pieces to Close the Intelligence Gap.* Hoboken, NJ: John Wiley & Sons, 2004.

Collins, Jim. *Good to Great: Why Some Companies Make the Leap…And Others Don't.* New York: Harper Business, 2001.

Collins, Jim. "Best New Year's Resolution? A 'Stop Doing' List." *USA Today,* December 30, 2003.

Committee of Sponsoring Organizations of the Treadway Commission. "Effective Enterprise Risk Oversight: The Role of the Board of Directors." www.coso.org.

Committee of Sponsoring Organizations of the Treadway Commission. *Enterprise Risk Management – Integrated Framework*, Executive Summary. Committee of Sponsoring Organizations of the Treadway Commission, 2004.

Damodaran, Aswath. *Strategic Risk Taking: A Framework for Risk Management.* San Francisco, CA: Wharton School Publishing, 2008.

Dreyer, S., and David Ingram. "Enterprise Risk Management: Standard & Poor's to Apply Enterprise Risk Analysis to Corporate Ratings." New York: Standard & Poor's, 2008.

Epstein, Marc J., and Bill Birchard. *Counting What Counts: Turning Corporate Accountability to Competitive Advantage.* Reading, MA: Perseus Books Group, 2000.

Epstein, Marc J., and Jean-François Manzoni. "The Balanced Scorecard and *Tableau de Bord*: Translating Strategy into Action." *Management Accounting,* January 1992, 28–36.

Epstein, Marc J., and Marie-Josée Roy. "How Does Your Board Rate?" *Strategic Finance,* February 2004, 24–31.

Epstein, Marc J., and Marie-Josée Roy. "Measuring and Improving the Performance of Corporate Boards." The Society of Management Accountants of Canada, 2001. http://www.cma-canada.org/index.cfm?ci_id=4614&la_id=1.

Epstein, Marc J., and Priscilla S. Wisner. "Increasing Corporate Accountability: The External Disclosure of Balanced Scorecard Measures." *Balanced Scorecard Report,* July–August 2001, 10–13.

Epstein, M. J., and M. J. Roy. "Measuring and improving the performance of corporate boards using the Balanced Scorecard." *Balanced Scorecard Report,* March–April 2003, 12–15.

Frigo, Mark. L. *A Balanced Scorecard for Internal Auditing Departments.* Altamonte Springs, FL: The Institute of Internal Auditors Research Foundation, 2002.

Frigo, Mark L. and Richard J. Anderson. "Embracing Enterprise Risk Management: Practical Approaches for Getting Started," New York: Committee of Sponsoring Organizations of the Treadway Commission (COSO), 2011. www.coso.org.

Frigo, Mark. L. "Mission Driven Strategy." *Strategic Finance,* August 2003, 8–11.

Frigo, Mark. L. "Performance Measures that Drive the First Tenet of Business Strategy." *Strategic Finance,* September 2003, 8–11.

Bibliography

Frigo, Mark L. "Performance Measures that Drive the Goal Tenets of Strategy." *Strategic Finance,* October 2003, 9–11.

Frigo, Mark L. "Return Driven: Lessons from High Performance Companies." *Strategic Finance,* July 2008, 25–30.

Frigo, Mark L. "Strategic Risk Assessment," chapter 6 in *Strategic Risk Management Implementation Guide.* Risk and Insurance Management Society, 2013. http://www.rims.org/aboutRIMS/Newsroom/News/Pages/StrategicRiskMngmntImplGuide2012.aspx.

Frigo, Mark L. "Strategy-Focused Performance Measures." *Strategic Finance,* September 2002, 10–15.

Frigo, Mark L. "Strategy and the Balanced Scorecard." *Strategic Finance,* November 2002, 6–9.

Frigo, Mark L. "Strategic Risk Management: The New Core Competency." *Balanced Scorecard Report.* Harvard Business Publishing, January–February 2009.

Frigo, Mark L. "Strategy-Focused Performance Measures." *Strategic Finance,* September 2002, 10–15.

Frigo, Mark. L. "The Balanced Scorecard Report" in *The State of Strategic Performance Measurement: The IMA 2001 Survey.* Boston, MA: Harvard Business Publishing Newsletters, 2001, 13–14.

Frigo, Mark L. "The Balanced Scorecard: 20 Years and Counting." *Strategic Finance,* October 2012, 49–53.

Frigo, Mark L. "The Balanced Scorecard and Strategy Maps: A Primer for Management Teams." The Conference Board (July 2012). https://www.conference-board.org/retrievefile.cfm?filename=TCB-DN-V4N15-12.pdf&type=subsite.

Frigo, Mark L. *The Impact of Business Process Reengineering on Internal Auditing.* Altamonte Springs, FL: The Institute of Internal Auditors Research Foundation, 1995.

Frigo, Mark L. "The Value of Strategy Maps." *Strategic Finance,* March 2004, 23–25.

Frigo, Mark L. "What Is Mission Driven Strategy?" *Strategic Finance,* August 2003, 8–11.

Frigo, Mark L., and Hans Læssøe. "Strategic Risk Management at the LEGO Group." *Strategic Finance,* February 2012, 27–35.

Frigo, Mark L., and Joel Litman. *DRIVEN: Business Strategy, Human Actions and the Creation of Wealth.* Strategy & Execution, 2008.

Frigo, Mark L., and Joel Litman. "What Is Return Driven Strategy?" *Strategic Finance,* February 2002, 11-13.

Frigo, Mark L., and Kip Krumwiede. "Balanced Scorecards: A Rising Trend in Strategic Performance Measurement." *Journal of Strategic Performance Measurement,* February-March 1999.

Frigo, Mark L., and Kip R. Krumwiede. "The Balanced Scorecard." *Strategic Finance,* January 2000, 50-54.

Frigo, Mark L., and Richard J. Anderson. "A Strategy Framework for Governance, Risk, and Compliance." *Strategic Finance,* February 2009, 20-61.

Frigo, Mark L., and Richard J. Anderson. "Strategic GRC: 10 Steps to Implementation." *Internal Auditor,* June 2009, 33-37.

Frigo, Mark L., and Richard J. Anderson. "Strategic Risk Assessment: A First Step for Risk Management and Governance." *Strategic Finance,* December 2009, 25-33.

Frigo, Mark L., and Richard J. Anderson. *Strategic Risk Management: A Primer for Directors. Director Notes.* The Conference Board 2012. https://www.conference-board.org/retrievefile.cfm?filename=TCB-DN-V4N15-12.pdf&type=subsite.

Frigo, Mark L., and Richard J. Anderson. "Strategic Risk Management: A Foundation for Enterprise Risk Management and Governance." *Journal of Corporate Accounting and Finance,* March-April 2011, 81-88.

Frigo, Mark L., and Richard J. Anderson. "Strategic Risk Assessment: A First Step for Improving Risk Management and Governance." *Strategic Finance,* December 2009, 25-33.

Frigo, Mark L., and Richard J. Anderson. "What Is Strategic Risk Management?" *Strategic Finance,* April 2011, 21-61.

Frigo, Mark L., and Richard J. Anderson. "10 Steps to Implement the Strategic GRC Framework." *Internal Auditor,* June 2009, 33-37.

Frigo, Mark L., Robert Paladino, and Larry Cuy, "Missed Opportunities in Performance and Enterprise Risk Management." *Journal of Corporate Accounting and Finance,* March-April 2009.

Frigo, Mark L., and Venkat Ramaswamy. "Co-Creating Strategic Risk-Return Management." *Strategic Finance,* May 2009, 25-33.

Hamel, Gary, and C. K. Prahalad. "Strategic Intent." *Harvard Business Review* 67, no. 3 (May 1989): 63-78.

Bibliography

Imperatives for Change: The IIA's Global Internal Audit Survey in Action: A Component of the CBOK Study. Altamonte Springs, FL: The Institute of Internal Auditors Research Foundation, 2011.

IIA Practice Guide, Developing the Internal Audit Strategic Plan. Altamonte Springs, FL: The Institute of Internal Auditors, July 2012.

Kaplan, Robert S., Anette Mikes, Robert Simons, Peter Tufano, and Michael Hofmann. "Managing Risk in the New World." *Harvard Business Review* 87, no. 10 (October 2009): 68–75.

Kaplan, Robert S. "The Balanced Scorecard and Nonprofit Organizations." *Balanced Scorecard Report,* November–December 2002.

Kaplan, Robert S. "Risk Management and the Strategy Execution System." *Balanced Scorecard Report,* 2009.

Kaplan, Robert S., and David P. Norton. *Alignment: Using the Balanced Scorecard to Create Corporate Synergies.* Boston, MA: Harvard Business School Press, 2006.

Kaplan, Robert S., and David P. Norton. "Building a Strategy Focused Organization." *Balanced Scorecard Report,* September–October 1999, 1–6.

Kaplan, Robert S., and David P. Norton. "Double-Loop Management: Making Strategy a Continuous Process." *Harvard Business Review* 78, no. 4 (July–August 2000): 1–4.

Kaplan, Robert S., and David P. Norton. "Putting the Balanced Scorecard to Work." *Harvard Business Review* 71, no. 5 (September 1993): 134–147.

Kaplan, Robert S., and David P. Norton. "Using the Balanced Scorecard as a Strategic Management System." *Harvard Business Review* 74, no. 1 (January–February 1996): 75–85.

Kaplan, Robert S., and David P. Norton. "Having Trouble with Your Strategy? Then Map It." *Harvard Business Review* 78, no. 5 (September–October 2000): 167–176.

Kaplan, Robert S., and Norton, David. P. "Linking the Balanced Scorecard to Strategy." *California Management Review* 39, no.1 (Fall 1996): 53–79.

Kaplan, Robert S., and Anette Mikes. "Managing Risk: A New Framework." *Harvard Business Review* 90, no. 6 (June 2012): 48–60.

Kaplan, Robert S., and David P. Norton. "Strategy Maps." *Strategic Finance,* March 2004, 35.

Kaplan, Robert S., and David P. Norton. *Strategy Maps: Converting Intangible Assets into Tangible Outcomes.* Boston, MA: Harvard Business School Press, 2004.

Kaplan, Robert S., and David P. Norton. "The Balanced Scorecard: Measures that Drive Performance." *Harvard Business Review,* January–February 1992, 71–79.

Kaplan, Robert S., and David P. Norton. *The Balanced Scorecard: Translating Strategy into Action.* Boston, MA: Harvard Business School Press, 1996.

Kaplan, Robert S., and David P. Norton. *The Execution Premium: Linking Strategy to Operations for Competitive Advantage.* Boston, MA: Harvard Business School Press, 2008.

Kaplan, Robert S., and David P. Norton. *The Strategy-Focused Organization: How Balanced Scorecard Companies Thrive in the New Business Environment.* Boston, MA: Harvard Business School Publishing, 2001.

Kaplan, Robert S., and David P. Norton. "The Office of Strategy Management." *Harvard Business Review,* October 2005, 72–80.

Kaplan, Robert S., and David P. Norton. "Using the Balanced Scorecard as a Strategic Management System." *Harvard Business Review,* January–February 1996, 75–85.

Kerr, Steve. "On the Folly of Hoping for A while Rewarding B." *Academy of Management Journal,* August 1988.

Lorsch, Jay W. "Smelling Smoke: Why Boards of Directors Need the Balanced Scorecard." *Balanced Scorecard Report,* September–October 2002, 9–11.

Merchant, Kenneth A. *Rewarding Results, Motivating Profit Center Managers.* Boston, MA: Harvard Business School Press, 1989.

Merchant, Kenneth A. "Evaluating General Managers' Performance." *Strategic Finance,* May 2007, 12–61.

Niven, P. R. *Balanced Scorecard Step by Step for Government and Nonprofit Agencies.* New York: John Wiley & Sons, 2002.

Niven, Paul R. *Balanced Scorecard Diagnostics: Maintaining Maximum Performance.* New York: John Wiley & Sons, 2005.

Niven, Paul R. *Balanced Scorecard Step by Step: Maximizing Performance and Maintaining Results.* New York: John Wiley & Sons, 2002.

Norton, David P. "Beware: The Unbalanced Scorecard." *Balanced Scorecard Report,* March–April 2000, 13–14.

Norton, David P. "Building Strategy Maps, Part Four: Organizing to Create Value." *Balanced Scorecard Report,* May–June 2001, 1–4.

Norton, David P. "The First Balanced Scorecard." *Balanced Scorecard Report,* March–April 2002, 15–16.

Norton, David P. "When a Scorecard Is Not a Scorecard." *Balanced Scorecard Report*, January–February 2000, 15–16.

Paladino, Bob. "How to Conduct a Balanced Scorecard Review to Create Strategic Alignment." *Balanced Scorecard Report*, November–December 2000, 12–14.

Porter, Michael E. "The Importance of Being Strategic." *Balanced Scorecard Report*, March–April 2002, 9–11.

Porter, Michael E. "What Is Strategy?" *Harvard Business Review* 74, no. 6 (November–December 1996): 61–78.

Porter, Michael E. *Competitive Advantage: Creating and Sustaining Superior Performance*. New York: Free Press, 1985.

Porter, Michael E. *Competitive Strategy: Techniques for Analyzing Industries and Competitors*. New York: Free Press, 1980.

Prahalad, C. K., and Gary Hamel. "The Core Competence of the Corporation." *Harvard Business Review* 68, no. 3 (May 1990): 79–91.

Reed, Brian, Erich Schumann, Princy Jain, and Rita Thakkar. IIA Practice Guide, Developing the Internal Audit Strategic Plan. Altamonte Springs, FL: The Institute of Internal Auditors, 2012. http://www.theiia.org/bookstore/product/practice-guide-developing-the-internal-audit-strategic-plan-download-pdf-1635.cfm.

Reichheld, Fred. *The Ultimate Question: Driving Good Profits and True Growth*. Boston, MA: Harvard Business School Press, 2006.

Rigby, Darrell. "Management Tools and Techniques." *California Management Review* 43, no. 2 (winter 2001): 139–159.

Risk-Based Strategy: Integrating Strategy Maps, Management Controls and Risk. American Institute of Certified Public Accountants, May 2011. http://www.aicpa.org/interestareas/businessindustryandgovernment/resources/erm/downloadabledocuments/risk_based_strategy_part_1_52711.pdf.

Sheehan, Norman T. "A Risk-Based Approach to Strategy Execution." *Journal of Business Strategy* 31, no. 5 (2010): 25–37.

Slywotzky, Adrian, and John Drzik. "Countering the Biggest Risk of All." *Harvard Business Review* 83, no. 4 (April 2005): 78–88.

Slywotzky, Adrian. *The Upside: The 7 Strategies for Turning Big Threats into Growth Breakthroughs*. New York: Crown Business, 2007.

Slywotzky, Adrian. "Finding the Upside Advantage of Downside Risk." *Strategic Finance*, November 2008, 8–61.

THE IIA RESEARCH FOUNDATION SPONSOR RECOGNITION

The Mission of The IIA Research Foundation is to shape, advance, and expand knowledge of internal auditing by providing relevant research and educational products to the profession globally. As a separate, tax-exempt organization, The Foundation depends on contributions from IIA chapters/institutes, individuals, and organizations. Thank you to the following donors:

STRATEGIC PARTNER

PRINCIPAL PARTNERS

THOMSON REUTERS
ACCELUS

DIAMOND PARTNERS (US $25,000+)

PLATINUM PARTNERS (US $15,000–$24,999)

GOLD PARTNERS (US $5,000–$14,999)

Stephen D. Goepfert, CIA, CRMA

SILVER PARTNERS (US $1,000–$4,999)

Anthony J. Ridley, CIA
Bonnie L. Ulmer
Edward C. Pitts
Hal A. Garyn, CIA, CRMA
IIA-Ak-Sar-Ben Chapter
IIA-Albany Chapter
IIA-Atlanta Chapter
IIA-Baltimore Chapter
IIA-Birmingham Chapter
IIA-Calgary Chapter
IIA-Central Illinois Chapter
IIA-Indianapolis Chapter
IIA-Lehigh Valley Chapter
IIA-Long Island Chapter
IIA-Miami Chapter
IIA-Northern California East Bay Chapter
IIA-Northwest Metro Chicago Chapter
IIA-Ocean State Chapter
IIA-Pittsburgh Chapter
IIA-Sacramento Chapter
IIA-San Antonio Chapter
IIA-San Gabriel Chapter
IIA-San Jose Chapter
IIA-Southern New England Chapter
IIA-St. Louis Chapter
IIA-Tidewater Chapter
IIA-Twin Cities Chapter
IIA-Vancouver Chapter
IIA-Western Carolinas Chapter
IIA-Wichita Chapter
Kevin M. Mayeux, CRMA
Margaret P. Bastolla, CIA, CRMA
Mark J. Pearson, CIA
Michael J. Palmer, CIA
Paul J. Sobel, CIA, CRMA
Richard F. Chambers, CIA, CCSA, CGAP, CRMA
Terri Freeman, CIA, CRMA
Urton L. Anderson, CIA, CCSA, CFSA, CGAP, CRMA
Wayne G. Moore, CIA

THE IIA RESEARCH FOUNDATION BOARD OF TRUSTEES

President
Frank M. O'Brien, CIA, *Olin Corporation*

Vice President-Strategy
Michael F. Pryal, CIA, *Federal Signal Corporation*

Vice President-Research and Education
Urton L. Anderson, PhD, CIA, CCSA, CFSA, CGAP,
University of Kentucky

Vice President-Development
Betty L. McPhilimy, CIA, CRMA,
Northwestern University

Treasurer
Mark J. Pearson, CIA, *Boise, Inc.*

Secretary
Scott J. Feltner, CIA, *Kohler Company*

Staff Liaison
Margie P. Bastolla, CIA, CRMA,
The Institute of Internal Auditors Research Foundation

Members

Neil D. Aaron, *News Corporation*

Fatimah Abu Bakar, CIA, CCSA, CRMA, *Columbus Advisory SDN BHD*

Audley L. Bell, CIA, *World Vision International*

Jean Coroller, *The French Institute of Directors*

Edward M. Dudley, CIA, CRMA, *ABB North America*

Philip E. Flora, CIA, CCSA, *FloBiz & Associates, LLC*

Steven E. Jameson, CIA, CCSA, CFSA, CRMA, *Community Trust Bank*

Jacques R. Lapointe, CIA, CGAP

James A. LaTorre, *PricewaterhouseCoopers LLP USA*

Kasurthrie Justine Mazzocco, *IIA-South Africa*

Guenther Meggeneder, CIA, CRMA, *ista International*

Larry E. Rittenberg, PhD, CIA, *University of Wisconsin*

Sakiko Sakai, CIA, CCSA, CFSA, CRMA, *Infinity Consulting*

Mark L. Salamasick, CIA, CRMA, *University of Texas at Dallas*

Jacqueline K. Wagner, CIA, *Ernst & Young LLP*

William C. Watts, CIA, CRMA, *Crow Horwath LLP*

THE IIA RESEARCH FOUNDATION COMMITTEE OF RESEARCH AND EDUCATION ADVISORS

Chairman
Urton L. Anderson, PhD, CIA, CCSA, CFSA, CGAP,
University of Kentucky

Vice Chairman
Frank M. O'Brien, CIA, *Olin Corporation*

Staff Liaison
Lillian McAnally,
The Institute of Internal Auditors Research Foundation

Members
Barry B. Ackers, CIA, *University of South Africa*
James A. Alexander, CIA, *Unitus Community Credit Union*
Sebastien Allaire, CIA, *Deloitte & Touche LLP (France)*
John Beeler, *SalesForce.com Inc.*
Karen Begelfer, CIA, CRMA, *Sprint Nextel Corporation*
Sharon Bell, CIA, *Wal-Mart Stores, Inc.*
Toby Bishop
Sezer Bozkus, CIA, CFSA, CRMA, *Grant Thornton Turkey*
John K. Brackett, CFSA, *McGladrey LLP*
Adil S. Buhariwalla, CIA, CRMA, *Emirates Airlines*
Richard R. Clune Jr., CIA, *Kennesaw State University*

Peter Funck, *Swedish Transport Administration*
Stephen G. Goodson, CIA, CCSA, CGAP, CRMA,
Texas Department of Public Safety
Ulrich Hahn, PhD, CIA, CCSA, CGAP
Karin L. Hill, CIA, CGAP, CRMA,
Texas Department of Assistive and Rehabilitative Services
Warren Kenneth Jenkins Jr., CIA, *Lowe's Companies, Inc.*
Jie Ju, *Nanjing Audit University*
Brian Daniel Lay, CRMA, *Ernst & Young LLP*
David J. MacCabe, CIA, CGAP, CRMA
Steve Mar, CFSA, *Nordstrom*
Jozua Francois Martins, CIA, CRMA, *Citizens Property Insurance Corporation*
John D. McLaughlin, *BDO*
Deborah L. Munoz, CIA, *CalPortland Cement Company*
Jason Philibert, CIA, CRMA, *TriNet*
Charles T. Saunders, PhD, CIA, CCSA, *Franklin University*
Rui Bezerra Silva, *Ventura Petroleo S.A.*
Tania Stegemann, CIA, CCSA, *Leighton Holdings Limited*
Warren W. Stippich Jr., CIA, CRMA, *Grant Thornton Chicago*
Deanna F. Sullivan, CIA, *SullivanSolutions*
Jason Thogmartin, *GE Capital Internal Audit*
Dawn M. Vogel, CIA, CRMA, *Great Lakes Higher Education Corporation*
Paul L. Walker, *St. John's University*
David Williams, *Dallas County Community College*
Valerie Wolbrueck, CIA, CRMA, *Lennox International, Inc.*
Douglas E. Ziegenfuss, PhD, CIA, CCSA, CRMA, *Old Dominion University*